FREEDOM HIGH

a play by

Adam Kraar

This play is a work of fiction, inspired by actual events during 'Freedom Summer' in 1964. The leading characters do not represent actual persons.

FREEDOM HIGH was first presented by Queens College and Queens Theatre in the Park, opening on May 9, 2007. It was directed by Susan Einhorn.

FREEDOM HIGH was subsequently produced by Uprooted Theatre in Milwaukee, Wisconsin, opening on November 18, 2014. It was directed by Marti Gobel.

The play spins out from Jessica's memories and impressions. Some actors will play more than one role; a non-literal, improvisational quality to the shifting of roles is desirable. This quality is especially important for the Volunteer Chorus. Even if a larger cast is used, the style of the production should not be documentary realism.

ALL RIGHTS RESERVED
Original Works Publishing

CAUTION: Professionals and amateurs are hereby warned that this play is subject to royalty. It is fully protected by Original Works Publishing, and the copyright laws of the United States. All rights, including professional, amateur, motion pictures, recitation, lecturing, public reading, radio broadcasting, television, and the rights of translation into foreign languages are strictly reserved.

Amateur and professional live stage performance rights to this play are controlled by Original Works Publishing and royalty arrangements and licenses must be secured well in advance of presentation. PLEASE NOTE that amateur royalty fees are set upon application in accordance with your producing circumstances. When applying for a royalty quotation and license please give us the number of performances intended, dates of production, your seating capacity and admission fee. Royalties are payable with negotiation from Original Works Publishing.

Royalty of the required amount must be paid whether the play is presented for charity or gain and whether or not admission is charged. Particular emphasis is laid on the question of amateur or professional readings, permission and terms for which must be secured from Original Works Publishing through direct contact.

Copying from this book in whole or in part is strictly forbidden by law, and the right of performance is not transferable.

Whenever the play is produced the following notice must appear on all programs, printing, and advertising for the play:

"Produced by special arrangement with
Original Works Publishing.
www.originalworksonline.com"

Due authorship credit must be given on all programs, printing and advertising for the play.

Freedom High
© Adam Kraar
Trade Edition, 2015
ISBN 978-1-63092-066-1

Also Available From Original Works Publishing

How to Make a Rope Swing by Shawn Fisher

Synopsis: Delores Wright is the wealthy town matriarch and former elementary school principal and Bo Wells is the custodian who worked under her strict supervision for most of his life. When they find themselves stranded together in the old condemned schoolhouse, their reunion takes a dark turn and they relive their first meeting, decades earlier. It was 1952, when some schools were first integrated in this region nicknamed the "Mississippi of the North". Bo's wife, the school's first black teacher, was found drowned in a nearby river, hanging by her ankle from an old rope swing after it was rumored she had struck a white child. The papers dismissed it as an accident resulting from the "wild and drunken actions of a young colored woman". When Mrs. Wright reveals that she has dreams about the incident, Bo suspects she knows more than she admits. As the night grows colder and the failing health of Mrs. Wright becomes increasingly evident, Bo tries to understand his wife's final moments and Mrs. Wright's role in her death.

Cast Size: 1 Senior Male, 1 Senior Female, 1 Male (20s)

CAST

At minimum, the play requires three women (including one African-American) and four men (including two African-Americans), though a larger cast – up to sixteen actors – is possible. Doubling can be used freely.

Below is a suggested doubling plan, although certainly not the only way it could be done:

JESSICA, a white woman, 21

JOHN, a white man, 20's (could double as Citizen One)

HELEN, a white woman, 20's (could double as Rita Schwerner)

RAY WOODS, a white man, 36 (could double as Young Man and Citizen Two)

ROSALIND, an African-American woman, could double as Fannie Lou Hamer

HENRY, an African-American man, 26

BOB MOSES, 29, an African-American man, doubles as two Ministers and other roles (such as Militant Staff Member and Farmer)

The actors playing John, Helen, and Young Man can also become the VOLUNTEER CHORUS representing a cross-section of the four hundred volunteers as well as miscellaneous small roles (Reporters, a Congregation, a Boy, etc.)

TIME: 1964

PLACE: Western College in Oxford, Ohio

SET: A simple unit set will suggest multiple locations. Shifts of location are probably best achieved, for the most part, by the use of lighting changes and sound cues. Additional 'cues' about location are conveyed through the dialogue.

HISTORICAL NOTES

The major events of the week of June 21, 1964 depicted in the play – including the disappearance of James Chaney, Andrew Goodman, Mickey Schwerner – represent historical fact. The public speeches of Bob Moses in the play are essentially drawn from his actual speeches.

The play takes liberties with the historical record in several small ways. For dramatic purposes, I've expanded the length of time in which there was uncertainty about whether the Project would proceed. My aim is to honor the actual persons involved while also creating a theatre piece that conjures up the dramatic spirit of this story.

FREEDOM HIGH

ACT ONE

(AT RISE, JESSICA stands, center stage, with a far-away look in her eyes.

JESSICA is a white woman, 21. She is not precisely 'pretty,' yet she has piercing eyes, mischievous eye-brows, sensual lips, long arms and legs, and a boldness that can, at times, be very appealing. She wears a denim skirt and a simple sleeveless blouse with a paper name tag on it.

The LIGHT on her intensifies. SHE shakes her head, and addresses the audience:)

JESSICA: Here I am! Surrounded by people I've dreamed of being with for four years.
 ...And I've never felt more alone. ... I've gone without sleep before, that's not it. I keep re-enacting all the encounters I had today, as if I missed something really important...

(She acts out one of her encounters.)

"Hello, I'm Jessica Kuplevsky, from Baltimore and Cambridge, and I'm here because... I need to do something about the hatred that's..."

(A VOLUNTEER wearing a backpack appears and addresses JESSICA.)

DISILLUSIONED VOLUNTEER: You really want to help people?

JESSICA *(to the audience)* This guy from Stanford. He'd been here the week before. I think he'd bombed out of training.

DISILLUSIONED VOLUNTEER: Pack your bags and get out of here.

JESSICA *(to the Volunteer)* Listen: They put this together in a just a few months. But look around you. Young people from every major university. Leaders from the Movement, lawyers, ministers, the press. Of course it's a little chaotic – it's like a revolution.

DISILLUSIONED VOLUNTEER: You have no idea what's—

JESSICA: Listen!

(A WOMAN is heard humming.)

DISILLUSIONED VOLUNTEER: *(cynically)* Oh, they sing beautifully about love and—

JESSICA: That's Fannie Lou Hamer. She tried to register – her family got kicked off their farm. She's got permanent injuries from the beatings—

DISILLUSIONED VOLUNTEER: They're just sending you down there to get killed, for the publicity.

JESSICA: That's—!

DISILLUSIONED VOLUNTEER: I guarantee you: volunteers are gonna get lynched.

(The DISILLUSIONED VOLUNTEER exits. ANOTHER VOLUNTEER appears.)

ANOTHER VOLUNTEER:
The rope cutting into your neck
You can't breathe
You can't scream.

(OTHER VOLUNTEERS APPEAR. They all wear name tags, and look collegiate. THEY address each other.)

VARIOUS VOLUNTEERS: — Just because you tried to vote
— Because you're black
— For God's sake, it's 1964. The Civil War's been over for 99 years!
— I heard, in McComb County—
— It's hot down there.
— Primordial.

JESSICA: *(fervently, with mixed emotions)* Mississippi! ...In six days I leave this sheltered campus for Mississippi.

(The LIGHTS CHANGE: We hear birds, the strumming of a guitar, and then singing. We – and JESSICA – become aware of the campus of Western College in Ohio. Trees. Perhaps the corner of an old dorm. STUDENT VOLUNTEERS gather, introduce themselves to each other, and sit down on the lawn. Among them are JOHN and HELEN.

FANNIE LOU HAMER, an African-American woman, appears and continues singing. JESSICA joins in, and then so does HELEN. JOHN plays along on his guitar. Then FANNIE LOU HAMER addresses the VOLUNTEERS.)

FANNIE LOU HAMER: If you all are goin' down to Mississippi, you gonna need to sing, and not just sittin' on your fannies. You need to get up on your feet – come on!

(The VOLUNTEERS stand up.)

FANNIE LOU HAMER: You need to fill your lungs, and sing like your life depended on it. 'Cause when you get down to Mississippi, there'll be times when your life does depend on your ability to sing. Now lemme hear you.

(The VOLUNTEERS sing adequately.)

FANNIE LOU HAMER: This is a Movement, people, you got to move. And clap your hands. You got to feel it. Show me what you can really do.

(The VOLUNTEERS sing more energetically, though without much soul. FANNIE LOU HAMER joins them, and injects more energy into their song. The LIGHTS CHANGE – a fantasy – spotlighting JESSICA and FANNIE LOU HAMER.)

JESSICA: Mrs. Hamer, where did you find your courage?

FANNIE LOU HAMER: Nothin' I did. It all comes from the good Lord.

JESSICA: But how? How do you reach... the Lord?

FANNIE LOU HAMER: Why, child, you pray. You sing, and pray, and just believe. You just believe. He will come into your life.

JESSICA: But, you see, I wasn't raised with religion. My father is a scientist.

FANNIE LOU HAMER: What about your mother?

JESSICA: She died when I was ten.

FANNIE LOU HAMER: Poor child. But you must have faith to come here, and devote your summer to helping the folks in Mississippi. I can see you have such love in your heart.

JESSICA: I do, I do, but it's all mixed up with...

(The LIGHTS abruptly change: we see the whole group. The singing resumes.)

FANNIE LOU HAMER: *(singing)* "I'm gonna let it shine! Let it shine, let it shine, let it shine!"

JESSICA: Mrs. Hamer!

FANNIE LOU HAMER: Sing it, chirrun!

(The VOLUNTEERS sing, then hum. JESSICA speaks to the audience.)

JESSICA: Our singing improved, but it lacked... soul. Soul! If only I could've talked to Fannie. But so much was happening. And behind all the talk and the singing and the earnest expressions, I could see: each one of us was here for a different reason:

VARIOUS VOLUNTEERS: *(coming forward and assuming different roles.)*
—I'm here because of John F. Kennedy. One day I plan to be President, and guide this country to greater vistas of freedom.
—I'm here 'cause of that bombing in Birmingham. Four little girls killed, and for what?
—I'm here 'cause I really dig the blues – gonna go to Mississippi and get the blues in my blood.
—I'm here because we must change the economic, governmental, and religious foundations of this imperialistic oligarchy.
—I'm here because my life is about service to Jesus Christ.
—I'm here because I really, really need a girlfriend.

(The VOLUNTEERS and FANNIE LOU HAMER exit, singing, and JESSICA is alone.)

JESSICA: I wanted to become involved with the Movement ever since I saw the photographs of those young men sitting in at the lunch counter in North Carolina. They had a seriousness, a focus, that I'd never seen before. Meanwhile, my father expected I'd get my Master's degree, teach for a year, then get married and have three kids. He thinks I'm out of my mind to come here. There's so much he doesn't know about me. There's so much no one knows about me. Including myself. I leap first, and ask questions later. I've had sex with men I didn't know very well, sometimes didn't really like, and I've enjoyed it. But that's not relevant anymore. I'm not here to chase my appetites, or improve my mind. I'm here... to do something for others, for this country of ours. Because this country is... like me. Parts are stunningly beautiful, young, full of promise. And parts have these deep scars that barely cover the most horrible... It's so late I don't even know what I'm saying.

...I shouldn't have thrown myself at him. But seeing him walk down the path, after months of thinking about him and Mississippi... like a dream.

(LIGHTS SHIFT: A path on campus. HENRY enters, carrying a large stack of papers and folders, looking preoccupied. HENRY is African-American, about 25. He is on the short side, stocky, dark-skinned. He's handsome in a simple, earthy way, with the modest expression of a reserved person. At times, he might almost seem stiff. His eyes, however, reveal an intense fierceness.)

JESSICA: Henry? Henry!

(JESSICA runs up to him.)

HENRY: 'Scuse me?

JESSICA: It's Jessica – Jessica Kuplevsky. You spoke at Harvard?

HENRY: Yes, but I—

JESSICA: It's because of you that I'm here. You talked about how they bombed that farmer's house. I'd really like to work in your county, registering people.

HENRY: I have nothin' to do with— [deciding who goes where]

JESSICA: May I help you...? [carry those folders]

HENRY: No. Thanks. I got to—

JESSICA: Are you okay? You look different somehow. I brought a lot of canned meat, in case—

HENRY: I gotta move on, miss.

JESSICA: Jessica. Let me—

HENRY: That's not—

JESSICA: I'll just take—

HENRY: No—

JESSICA: Just a few—

(Between JESSICA's trying to take some of the papers, and HENRY's resistance, much of the stack of papers falls.)

JESSICA: Oh, shoot! Sorry! Let me—

HENRY: Just leave it. You hear me? Just leave it.

JESSICA: But...

HENRY: I don't need your help! Don't want your help! Just go. You hear me? Sometimes it's better, just let people help themself. – Shit!

JESSICA: I'm sorry.

(After a moment, JESSICA leaves HENRY's area. SHE practically runs into RAY WOODS. RAY is white, 36, dressed in brown slacks and a white short-sleeve shirt. HE carries a large, weathered-looking Bible.)

RAY: Hey. Hello. You're lookin' awful serious for someone who's not yet in Mississippi.

JESSICA: Oh.

RAY: Ray Woods, National Council of Churches.

(RAY offers her hand, and they shake. HE holds on to her hand for a long time.)

JESSICA: Jessica. Kuplevsky.

RAY: Russian-Jewish.

JESSICA: How did you—?

RAY: My second freedom ride, I sat next to a guy called Nathan Rudevsky, son of a Russian Jew.

JESSICA: You went on freedom rides?

RAY: Eight of 'em. Woulda gone on more, 'cept I had a little encounter in Montgomery with a lead pipe.

(Finally letting go of her hand, RAY points to a scar on his temple.)

JESSICA: Oh my God.

RAY: You wanna touch it? *(beat)* Jessica Kuplevsky.

JESSICA: You're a minister.

RAY: I am. But some-a my best friends are Jews. That's a joke, by the way.

JESSICA: Ah! *(pause)* I wanted to go on the freedom rides.

RAY: So now you're on your way down to the Delta.

JESSICA: Have you been?

RAY: Only a few days here and there. But, as you may have guessed, I'm a product of the South. I'm thoroughly familiar with the mind of the Delta racist. You know, at heart, they're simply scared and confused. Just like the rest of us, right?

JESSICA: *(looking around the campus)* ...It's not quite what I...

RAY: Tell me. What did you expect?

JESSICA: Oh, it's just my usual dewy-eyed—

RAY: I could really use some dewy-eyed naiveté right about now. Please.

JESSICA: I just didn't expect everybody – well, the whites – to be so... The way they are in Cambridge. So cool. Articulate, but contained. Like young Democrats at a fund-raising picnic.

RAY: Yeah.

JESSICA: And I've barely had a chance to talk with any of the Negroes. Not that I expect them to be grateful or anything, it's just...

RAY: People gotta sniff each other out. No one wants to be the first to be uncool. So it's all up to you.

JESSICA: What do you mean?

RAY: Someone's gotta stand up and just speak their heart. Without correctness, or coolness, or tact, or moderation. Otherwise, nothin' gets done. And I got a feeling, you're elected for the job.

(LIGHTS CHANGE. JESSICA, alone, speaks to the audience.)

JESSICA: Ray has a sparkling madness in his eyes. He sees something in me. What does he see? ...I must get some sleep. Tomorrow the training begins.

(BLACKOUT. We hear a large crowd talking. Moments later, LIGHTS COME UP and the stage represents The Auditorium. Behind a podium, there is a blackboard with a map of Mississippi in chalk. BOB MOSES stands next to the podium, addressing the audience.

MOSES is the leader of the Summer Project. HE wears overalls, but with his glasses, his reserve, his probing intellectual demeanor, he sometimes seems like a young philosophy professor – until we see the deepness of his commitment.

We also see a section of the audience, where some volunteers sit or stand (this area could be situated among the audience of the theatre, suggesting that the audience are volunteers). Among the volunteers are JESSICA, JOHN, and HELEN.)

BOB MOSES: This area is Klan territory. No one – none of you – will be safe in this area. The violence is untamed, ugly, irrational. If you asked one of the Klansmen why, he'd probably say "We've got to keep the nigger in his place." ...Five Negroes have been murdered since the beginning of the year.

(Pause)

JOHN: This guy is strange.

JESSICA: Ssh.

JOHN: The way he keeps pausing?

JESSICA: He's gauging our response.

BOB MOSES: The response to these killings? The local authorities sometimes go through the motions of an investigation. But there has not been one indictment. And there is not likely to be, unless....

JOHN: *(to Jessica)* ...Unless what?

JESSICA: Ssh!

BOB MOSES: When you come down South this summer, you bring with you the eyes and ears of the country. We have been asking the Federal government to bring in the FBI for three years. We appealed to President Kennedy, we've tried to talk with President Johnson.

(MOSES pauses for a long time. JOHN nudges JESSICA, as if to say, 'What is this?')

JESSICA: He's thinking.

JOHN: He's staring at his shoes.

JESSICA: John, please.

BOB MOSES: Our goals are limited. If you can go and come back alive, that is something. If you can go into Negro homes and just sit and talk, that will be a huge job. We're not thinking of integrating the lunch counters. The Negroes in Mississippi haven't the money to eat in those places anyway.

(*Pause. The DISILLUSIONED VOLUNTEER from Stanford enters, with his backpack, and takes a seat behind JESSICA and JOHN.*)

BOB MOSES: There is an analogy in *The Plague* by Camus. The country isn't willing yet to admit it has the plague, but it pervades the whole society.

(*ROZ, an African-American woman in her twenties, and HENRY enter the auditorium, looking very agitated.*)

HENRY: I think we gotta do it now.

ROZ: Wait.

HENRY: He's got to know.

ROZ: Henry, he's in the middle of...

JESSICA: Something's happening.

(*HENRY gestures to MOSES, who comes to the edge of the stage. HENRY and ROZ whisper to MOSES.*)

DISILLUSIONED VOLUNTEER: See, I told you: complete disorganization.

JESSICA: You're still here?

DISILLUSIONED VOLUNTEER: My ride doesn't leave till two. There's room for one more.

JOHN: Ssh. (*points to the stage*)

(*ROZ and HENRY have finished talking to MOSES, and leave. MOSES comes back center stage, and looks down at his feet. A long pause. Finally, MOSES looks out at the audience.*)

BOB MOSES: Yesterday morning, three of our people left Meridian, Mississippi, to investigate a church burning in Neshoba County. They haven't come back, and we haven't had any word from them. We spoke to John Doar in the Justice Department. He promised to order the FBI to act, but the local FBI still says they have been given no authority.

(MOSES wanders off to the side of the area, lost in thought. We hear many people in the auditorium talking.)

HELEN: You think they were volunteers?

DISILLUSIONED VOLUNTEER: I know who they were. I heard the staff in the cafeteria. They were here last week. One was a volunteer, from my group.

HELEN: Oh my God.

DISILLUSIONED VOLUNTEER: His name was Andy. Smart kid, very energetic. Jewish.

JESSICA: So what if he was Jewish? – is Jewish. We don't know what happened.

DISILLUSIONED VOLUNTEER: Haven't you been listening? If someone disappears, it means one thing.

HELEN: Maybe they had car trouble.

DISILLUSIONED VOLUNTEER: Come on. They took Andy down there, and they got him killed.

JESSICA: Hey – assuming the worst—

JOHN: *(completing Jessica's thought)* No one said this was gonna be summer camp.

DISILLUSIONED VOLUNTEER: You want to be a martyr? You may feel differently with a rope around your neck.

JESSICA: Look, I'm sorry you had a bad week of training. I'm sorry you weren't welcomed with open arms—

DISILLUSIONED VOLUNTEER: I just hate to see you people get yourselves killed. And for what?

JESSICA: ...I think you should leave now.

JOHN: ...Go on. Stanford.

DISILLUSIONED VOLUNTEER: What are you going to do? Drag me out, like a Mississippi Sheriff?

(After a moment, the DISILLUSIONED VOLUNTEER exits. Pause.)

HELEN: We need to do something.

JESSICA: *(coming forward)* But the air had gone out of the room. People wanted to escape, but didn't want to be seen as cowards. And Bob Moses... just stood there, staring into space. As if he was seeing another world.

(LIGHTS SHIFT: A SPOT on BOB MOSES, and another SPOT on JESSICA, watching him.)

BOB MOSES:
   I was responsible.
   The shooting of Jimmy Travis
   The beating of Herbert Lee
   The face of Louis Allen, scattered on the driveway
   Tears and blood, swallowed by the hot clay.
   "Speak up, testify, for only if we stand up can we make a change."

He stood up – and was pushed down into the earth.

Young men, moved by my words,
Became blind to their safety.

Children. Little more than children.
Looking at me like I have all the answers.
I tell them, no one can give you the answers.
When you are cornered by a beast
And next to you are children
No one can tell you what to do.

But I sent them down to Neshoba.
I pushed and nearly insisted,
"Bring down a thousand white students;
We need our white brothers and sisters
Working alongside of us"
Attracting the eyes and ears of a nation
Blind and deaf to the murder of Herbert Lee.

And now these kids, looking up to me.
Don't look up to me!
I do what I must do, and so must you.
If you only do what someone else intends
Your death will make your life meaningless.

How do I tell them this?
How can I make them see,
before they're pulled over
by Mississippi law
On a dark country road
And must face, all alone, the long... endless? ...night?

JESSICA: Mr. Moses? Bob? What can I do?

(Pause. BOB MOSES crosses to another part of the stage, sits and broods.)

JESSICA: He went to the porch of Peabody Hall and sat down, oblivious to everything around him. Sat there for the whole rest of the day. Is this project even possible?

(LIGHTS CHANGE: RITA SCHWERNER, a young white woman, gets up on the stage. Containing her fear with a wiry intensity, she erases most of the map of Mississippi, and writes:
"JAMES CHANEY – CORE STAFF
MICHAEL SCHWERNER – CORE STAFF
ANDREW GOODMAN – SUMMER PROJECT VOLUNTEER
NESHOBA COUNTY – DISAPPEARED")

RITA: *(addressing the audience)* I'm Rita Schwerner. My husband, Mickey, his co-worker, James Chaney, and Andrew Goodman, a Summer Project Volunteer, were arrested yesterday for speeding. Deputy Sheriff Cecil Price of Neshoba County claims that he released them last night, at 10 PM. ...But we have not heard from them. We called every jail in the area, but no one has seen them. We called the FBI in Jackson, but they keep saying they're not sure whether a Federal statute has been violated.

So this is what we need to do. We need to form into groups according to the areas that you come from, and wire your congressmen. Tell them what has happened, that the FBI is refusing to take action. And if the government does not act, then none of us are safe. None of us. ...We need to move quickly.

(RITA exits. LIGHTS SHIFT (though a spot remains on the blackboard with the names of the missing young men.)

(The VOLUNTEERS (including JESSICA) gather at a table, and compose telegrams. THEY play a variety of characters.)

VOLUNTEERS: *(severally)* —Dear Congressman,
—Dear Senator,
—Dear Harold,

ALL: I am a volunteer with the Mississippi Summer Project.

VOLUNTEERS: *(severally)* —A senior at Harvard University
—I recently graduated from Vassar
—My father is treasurer of your re-election campaign
—My mother went to Bryn Mayr with your mother

—A junior at Queens College
—I earned my Doctor of Divinity from Yale
—You may recall my uncle who was your professor at Columbia
—My father is chairman of the International Rubber Corporation

—Three Civil Rights workers
—Two of whom happen to be white
—Have gone missing in Mississippi

(BLACKOUT. Then- A DREAM: Sound of crickets, an owl. We hear a car screeching to a halt on a dirt road, then a couple of others. Doors slam. In the dark, voices.)

MAN'S VOICE: Come on, boy, you wanna see Mississippi? I'll show you Mississippi.

JESSICA'S VOICE: Where are we going?

MAN'S VOICE: You gonna see the real Mississippi. You wanna live with the niggers, you wanna love the niggers, well I'm gonna treat you just like a nigger.

(The stage is barely lit: faint moonlight, a flashlight – the black and grey shades of a nightmare. Two CITIZENS'

COUNCIL MEN enter dragging on a Freedom Project Volunteer (played by Jessica).)

JESSICA: Look, I think we got off on the wrong foot.

CITIZEN ONE: You do?

JESSICA: I can understand how you feel.

CITIZEN ONE: Oh, yeah? How do I feel?

JESSICA: You have a way of life, you've enjoyed for a long time. You don't mean anybody any harm, right? And then all these people come in and want to turn everything upside down. That would definitely be aggravating. Right?

CITIZEN TWO: Hey, Carl, we gonna listen to a lecture, or teach a lesson?

JESSICA: Listen, Carl—

(CARL hits JESSICA in the face with his flashlight, knocking her to the ground. JESSICA cries out.)

CITIZEN ONE: That's 'sir' to you, boy. Y'hear me? Answer me.

JESSICA: Please—

(CITIZEN ONE hits JESSICA again.)

CITIZEN ONE: You call me sir. Say it, nigger-lover.

(A YOUNG MAN's scream is heard offstage, then a shot.)

JESSICA: Oh God!

(Offstage, we hear HELEN scream.

LIGHTS SHIFT: The dorm at Western College. JESSICA runs to HELEN, who sits in a stairwell, gripping a blanket.)

JESSICA: Helen!

HELEN: Please... don't mind me...

(JESSICA sits down with HELEN and puts an arm around her. HELEN cries. JESSICA holds her.)

HELEN: ....This dream! ...'cept it wasn't a dream, it was...

JESSICA: Tell me.

HELEN: They drove us out of town, down this long, dark road... You think I'm— [crazy]

JESSICA: No. I had that dream too.

HELEN: Was Andrew Goodman in it?

JESSICA: *(remembering)* Yes. Yes.

HELEN: Oh, God! They hung him, didn't they?

JESSICA: Helen—

HELEN: I don't want to be hanged! I don't care if they shoot me, or...

JESSICA: We don't know what—

HELEN: You ever seen a picture of a man who's been hanged? It's like the life has been wrung outta him, bit by bit, till he's just this dry... Thing, twisting. Twisting, all twisted...

(HELEN puts her hand to her throat, sobs.)

JESSICA: Hey! Hey.

HELEN: I'm sorry! ...You're not scared, are you?

JESSICA: I was—

HELEN: You're so confident. So present. I've never been with a man. I've never really lived. I thought somehow this would be the beginning of my life, but... I don't know what to do! I can't drop out. Everyone in Richmond knows I'm here. And my Daddy, he was so against this. If I came home now, he'd be so angry. *(She laughs briefly.)* –But I really can't. Not now. The whole country's watchin' us.

(She clutches her blanket to her, rocks back and forth.)

LIGHTS SHIFT: *JESSICA addresses the audience.)*

JESSICA: Four A.M. again. Gonna hate myself in three hours. But how I can sleep? Those images! ...Except now, they don't seem real. Like the disappearance is just an object lesson created by the Project Leaders. *(beat)* They've assigned me to teach Freedom School. Not what I came for. I'd be so good at registering voters. I know, I can't say anything right now. ...I haven't really lived. I've dabbled, experimented, posed. And the staff, and Ray Woods – they're the real deal. ...I have to do *something*! *(pause)* Tomorrow we learn nonviolence.

(BLACKOUT. Sound of school desks being moved around.

LIGHTS UP on a Classroom. Also, upstage, we still see the blackboard with the names of the three missing young men. ROZ faces the audience. HENRY stands, learning against a wall. The VOLUNTEERS are downstage of ROZ.)

ROZ: My name is Rosalind Anderson. Everyone calls me Roz. I'm a staff associate for Snick – the Student Nonviolent Coordinating Committee - and I'm going to be leading this morning's session. This is Henry Watkins, who's going to be Project Director for Clarksdale, and he'll be leading the afternoon session.

JOHN: Um, Roz – John Holbrook, from Berkeley. Any news from...?

ROZ: About 50 staff people left here yesterday, and went down to Mississippi to help with the search. As soon as we hear anything, we'll let you know.

HELEN: What's going to happen if... they find them?

(pause)

ROZ: I don't know.

HENRY: These three aren't the first to go missing in Mississippi. And they won't be the last either.

ROZ: We'll do the best we can to prepare you, but... it's extremely dangerous—

HENRY: It's hell down there. People are gonna get—

ROZ: Henry, maybe you'd like to tell people about your background?

HENRY: ...I'm from a town called Mabley, in Jasper County. Bob Moses came in three years ago to try to get some people registered. ...Three years. You know how many people we got registered? None. Zero. You know how many black folks got beaten? Shot at? Disappeared? Thirty-eight, so far. ...Much as they hate me, they gonna hate you a lot worse.

(RAY WOODS stumbles into the classroom, wearing sunglasses. HE is clearly hungover.)

ROZ: 'Morning, Ray. Glad you could join us.

(RAY gives ROZ a kind of salute, then sits down in a chair near her, as if he is one of the presenters.)

RAY: Sorry I'm late.

ROZ: Ray is with the National Council of Churches. We've got ministers and rabbis available to talk with any of you. If you're having second thoughts about going, please: talk to them.

HENRY: There's no shame in changin' your mind. A lotta you probly should.

(ROZ gives HENRY a look.)

RAY: You know how it is when your rectum feels all scrunched up, like it wants to crawl back up into your intestines? Well, that's normal. If you're not feeling that, talk to me.

ROZ: Thank you, Ray.

RAY: You're welcome, honey. Gonna talk about love today?

ROZ: I hope so.

JOHN: When are we going to hurl epithets at each other, and learn how to curl up into a ball?

ROZ: This afternoon. But this morning, I'd like us to talk about... about love. Because the essence of nonviolence is love.

JOHN: Excuse me. I know I'm new. But we effectively lost a day yesterday. In five days, we leave for our assignments. It seems to me that the best use of this time—

ROZ: I've been doing direct action for four years, and the reason the sit-ins and the Freedom Rides were so successful was that we never separated our means from our ends. In five days, you're going to a place where there's an extraordinary amount of hate. So we need to talk about love.

JOHN: If we had four weeks... But let's face it. Like Henry said, we're heading into a war zone.

RAY: If you please – if I may. *(RAY stands up.)* Let me try to break this down for you all.
(HE takes off his sunglasses.) I was on a march in Smithtown, a floundering little burg 40 miles South of Raleigh. About 30 of us were there, protesting the refusal of the town to register Negroes. This young man, typical small-town redneck, leather jacket, slicked down hair, comes up to me, his eyes are clouded over with rage. He doesn't see me, he's probably really mad about his Daddy, who drinks too much and keeps him down. So this boy with a hint of stubble on his chin pushes me down onto the dusty asphalt, spits on me, and barks, "Get out of my town, nigger-lover." My first impulse – still – I wanna knock that sonofabitch down and show him what for. I still could, you know. But that's where love comes in. I look that boy in the eyes as I pick myself up and wipe his spit off my face. And that's when I think of Pete Robillard, my next door neighbor from when I was growin' up – when Pete was five, he was like a little angel, with the sweetest disposition you can imagine. And I can see, in the face of this Smithtown greaser, the cherubic cheeks and funny chin of 5-year-old Pete Robillard, and suddenly I'm smiling at this poor boy, almost huggin' him, 'cause he doesn't really know what he's doing. I say, "Which fountain here makes the best strawberry soda? Is it that one, or Rexall?"

"Wha?"

"You like strawberry or chocolate?"

"Uh, strawberry."

Now his friends are starin' at him, but he feels that I love somethin' in him that his grown-up pals never knew.

"So who makes the best one?" I ask.

"Rexall," he says. Then he looks at me real hard.

I say, "Thanks."

"For what?"

"I'm thirsty. Come have a soda with me."

JESSICA: *(impressed)* Damn!

HENRY: I wouldn't try that in Mississippi.

ROZ: Thank you, Ray. Thank you, Henry.

JESSICA: But what happened?

RAY: I didn't mean to—

JESSICA: Did he go with you?

RAY: Well, he looks at me. He considers it. Looks at his friends, who are lookin' at him. He gets that I could be a better friend than any-a those guys. But then he remembers, how he's gotta live in that town the rest of his life. So he walks away. He just departs the whole scene.

JESSICA: *(impressed)* That's...

RAY: It's simply using the power of love.

HENRY: Man, you don't have a clue. None a you get it! You go down there and try to give the Klan a little love? You gonna die real slow.

(Slight pause. LIGHTS SHIFT TO JESSICA, who speaks to the audience. Another LIGHT illuminates HENRY.)

JESSICA: Something's eating away at him. ...In three months, he's aged. In Cambridge, he was almost gangling, his complexion was bad. Now he's this gorgeous – perplexed – angry warrior. And he doesn't want us to be his troops, but feels like he's stuck with us. I must try to speak with him.

(The LIGHT on HENRY shifts to ROZ.)

JESSICA: ...And I love Roz. Rosalind Anderson. I love her like an older sister, or... She had each of us talk about love, and how love helped us through a personal crisis.

(Now LIGHTS come up more fully on the Classroom. The VOLUNTEERS and RAY stand and address the audience, as ROZ observes. HENRY stands to the side, brooding.)

VARIOUS VOLUNTEERS: — The Greeks called it... agape.
 — They padlocked our community center!
 — When I feel like throttling my father
 — Beyond your tidy, predictable, Judeo-Christian values
 — She betrayed me... in my own Buick!
 — The look on the face of that ancient Negro woman
 — The look my grandfather gave me, just before he died.

(The LIGHTS become more realistic.)

ROZ: John, are you with us?

(JOHN has been looking at something outside the window.)

JOHN: Something's happening out there.

ROZ: I think it's just the television crews.

JESSICA: The cameraman from NBC has a mad crush on John. He's destined to be the male face of Freedom Summer.

ROZ: Let's try to—

JOHN: I'll be right back.

(JOHN exits.)

ROZ: I'm sorry, Helen. Please go on.

(Pause)

HELEN: *(continuing a story)* Granddaddy was a remarkable man: tall and distinguished, with these eyes that saw all of you, and loved all of you. ...So when the doctor... shut his eyes, it was all over for me. I was done – done with this world. But then, the choir starts in with Bach's "Jesu, Joy of Man's Desire" – Granddad's favorite. And I opened my eyes and I could almost hear... Granddad's raspy voice, singin' along. I felt his eyes and I felt the eyes of Jesus, looking right through me to my heart, forgivin' me for being such a fool. The love of Jesus is a non-conditional love, and all we have to do is accept it, and it can get us through anything.

(RAY goes to HELEN and gives her a big, long hug. MUSIC: We hear a gospel choir humming "Jesu, Joy of Man's Desire." LIGHTS CHANGE: JESSICA addresses the audience.)

JESSICA: I know it sounds corny and desperate. But that's not how it was! It wasn't just a Jesus thing, or a Movement thing. Everybody felt it. Even Henry, I think – his face got younger, though he still wouldn't look at us. And Roz – Roz! – radiating this warmth, this hope, this belief in us. I think she believes in us more than we do!

(The MUSIC stops, and the LIGHTS become mostly focused on ROZ and JESSICA.)

ROZ: It's happening, it's really happening
　　　The good questions, the necessary doubts.
　　　The barriers come up, are shared, and then start to come down.
　　　The Beloved Community.

JESSICA: "The Beloved Community!" Yes!

ROZ: We will shine our lights
　　　Into Mississippi nights
　　　Until they turn to day.
　　　It is the muddy, bloody, necessary journey.
　　　In the end, we'll all join hands and sing.
　　　We will. We will. We will.
　　　Even Senator Eastland, and Governor Johnson.
　　　Even the Grand Klux...

JESSICA: This tear rolled down her cheek.
　　　She's not one for advertising her wounds.
　　　(Like Mom. Like Mom.)
　　　Holding in all that pain;
　　　She believes suffering is redemptive.
　　　(Unlike Dad, who thinks suffering
　　　　is to be avoided at all costs.)
　　　Roz is just a few years older than me.
　　　A lifetime of seeing her friends
　　　beaten and killed.
　　　She's so serious
　　　And yet
　　　So calm
　　　Like she's floating...
　　　She wears a wedding ring.

ROZ: *(to herself)* I know. I know.
　　　The Grand Klux won't hold my black hand.
　　　Won't join our circle.
　　　And my husband? Linwood?
　　　– Will you live to see it? *(beat)*

Where are you, Linwood?
Are you alive?
I wish you were here!
You might laugh at these kids,
but you couldn't hate them.
They would love you, and cry for you,
And want to give you their lives.
Are you with the three that... disappeared?
I hope, I pray, I beg you, Lord
Let him be alright.
Don't let them... smash...
His beautiful, powerful, stubborn head.

JESSICA: I love Roz. I love Ray. Even Henry, sort of.

ROZ: The Beloved Community.
We will, we are, we are making
The Beloved—

(Enter JOHN. LIGHTS CHANGE BACK TO NORMAL.)

JOHN: Listen: they found it. They found Mickey Schwerner's car. The Ford station wagon, all burnt up. They found it in a big creek outside Philadelphia, Mississippi.

JESSICA: And the three guys?

JOHN: They've been dragging the rivers, and scouring the woods, but no sign. ...It's going to be the lead story on every news show in the country.

(HENRY exits, JOHN follows him.)

RAY: *(quietly)* Let us pray.

(HELEN, ROZ and RAY bow their heads and silently pray. JESSICA watches them as the LIGHTS fade to black.)

In the darkness, we hear the following:)

HENRY'S VOICE: Coon!

ROZ'S VOICE: Ape!

HENRY'S VOICE: Nigger!

ROZ'S VOICE: Get outta the car, nigger!

(LIGHTS UP on the Classroom. JESSICA sits on some chairs arranged to look like the front seat of a car. HENRY and ROZ stand outside the 'car.' The other VOLUNTEERS watch, as HENRY and ROZ play the roles of white rednecks.)

HENRY: Are you deaf and black? I said get outta the car, nigger.

JESSICA: What did I do, Sheriff?

(HENRY yanks JESSICA out of the 'car' and throws her to the ground.)

HENRY: I tell you to speak? You don't speak a word till I tell ya to. Y'hear? ...You say, 'yes suh.' Say it!

JESSICA: *(somewhat sarcastically)* Yes, sir.

(HENRY spits on JESSICA. ROZ breaks out of the role-playing and addresses the group. As ROZ speaks, JESSICA gets up.)

ROZ: Okay. First mistake: the first thing you do when you get into a car is lock all the doors. Also, you want to learn all the roads, all the little dirt lanes off the main highway. If someone tries to pull you over, and you're not in town, you should strongly consider making a run for it. The last person who reported seeing Chaney, Goodman and Schwerner was the Sheriff who stopped them for speeding. We don't know for sure if that Sheriff was directly involved in their disappearance, but don't ever think that just because someone's in law enforcement they're not a threat to your life.

JOHN: Roz, Henry: Excuse me. I understand what you're trying to do, but is it really necessary to spit at us?

ROZ: Yes, it is. And we hate doing it. But please understand, the worst we do here is nothing compared to what you're going to face down there.

JOHN: Why not just show us the ropes? We're not children.

ROZ: John: ...I think you don't trust us.

JOHN: I'm simply making a—

ROZ: You don't want to work under Negro leadership, do you?

JOHN: That's... Obviously, if I signed up for this... Perhaps it'd be better if you and I spoke after. In the interests of time.

(Slight pause: ROZ considers how to handle this.)

HENRY: *(to Jessica)* I don't blame you bein' angry at me. But if you allow yourself to get angry at the wrong time down there...

ROZ: Everything – everything – depends on not giving in to hate. It's more than just a survival tactic—

(HENRY shakes his head.)

ROZ: I know Henry doesn't agree with me. But—

HENRY: We gotta move on. ...Let's review. The vital parts of your body? *(points to Helen.)*

HELEN: The neck, the head and the groin.

HENRY: How do we protect 'em? *(points to John.)*

JOHN: You curl up.

HENRY: You curl up like a baby. Keep your legs together, pull your knees up to your gut, you wanna be shielding your head and your neck with your hands and arms – like this. Okay? The other parts of your body can take a real beating before anything permanent goes wrong. *(HENRY picks up a broomstick.)* A billy club can make a real mess of your hands. Gonna get 'em all bloody. But they heal up. See? But your head... Your head gets caved in, it's not gonna heal up. Not ever.

(Pause: the VOLUNTEERS absorb what's facing them in Mississippi.)

ROZ: Shall we do the ATTACK scenario?

HENRY: *(nods.)* ...You— *(points to Jessica)* and you— *(points to Helen)* Stand up, please. Let's say you two are walking down Main Street, in Carthage, Mississippi. The streets are deserted. It's dusk. You all had to go to the store to get some powdered milk, 'cause they don't sell it on the side of town where you're staying. So... walk.

(HELEN and JESSICA walk.)

HENRY: You wanna walk like you know exactly where you're goin'. Try it.

(HELEN and JESSICA walk more purposefully. HENRY, still holding the broomstick, and ROZ, stand in their way. HENRY and ROZ assume the roles of rednecks.)

HENRY: Howdy, girls. Where y'all goin'?

JESSICA: We're, uh, goin' home.

ROZ: Home? Y'all gonna walk all the way to New York?

(JESSICA laughs.)

HENRY: *(dropping his redneck character)* Don't laugh!

JESSICA: I'm sorry, I just—

HENRY: There's gonna be a lot that you don't expect. I'm tellin' you all, that's how the people down there talk. You laugh—you blink—at the wrong time—

(HENRY brings the broomstick down into his hand. Pause. He resumes the role-playing:)

HENRY: Where y'all stayin'?

HELEN: Uh, we're guests of a family here in town.

HENRY: Guests? I ain't heard nothing about nobody havin' guests. Unless you two are guests of some niggers. Is that what you all are? Nigger-lovers? ...Answer me, girl.

HELEN: M-my name is Helen Graves. W-what's yours?

ROZ: Hank, I think we got us here two professional nigger-lovin' agitators.

HENRY: That what you are?

HELEN: No.

JESSICA: We're here to do some teaching.

ROZ: You're here to stir up trouble. We get along just fine in this town, we don't need any of your so-called teachin'. So why don't you pack up your Ivy League skirts and your beatnik tops and get on out of this town tonight. You hear me?

JESSICA: We don't want any trouble. Why don't you come visit our—?

ROZ: There ain't gonna be no Freedom School in Carthage, hear?

JESSICA: Do you even know what we do there?

HENRY: You oughta be ashamed, carryin' on like that with those black animals.

ROZ: We better not see you tomorrow. Do you understand me?

HELEN: Yes, I...

ROZ: Good. And you? You understand me?

JESSICA: I'd like to understand you better.

ROZ: Say what??

JESSICA: What are you so angry about?

(ROZ takes the broomstick from HENRY.)

ROZ: Listen to me: We give outside agitators a special one-way ticket. So I'm gonna ask you one last time, do you understand me?

HELEN: ...Yes, she does.

HENRY: You gonna be on the mornin' bus outta here?

(Pause)

JESSICA: This is our situation: There are 18 children—

HENRY: I must not-a heard you correctly. You are going to be on that bus tomorrow mornin'. Right?

JESSICA: Well, unless that bus is heading for the freedom school—

(ROZ suddenly pushes JESSICA to the ground. JESSICA curls up, somewhat. ROZ kicks JESSICA. HENRY breaks out of the role-playing.)

HENRY: *(as himself)* Jessica, what are you doing? What are you doing?

JESSICA: I'm protecting myself.

HENRY: You call that curlin' up like a baby?

JESSICA: Yeah.

HENRY: You're not protecting your groin. You wanna get kicked in your privates? And your elbows is stickin' out, you gonna get a broken arm. How many times I got to tell you: You need to get out of your head this idea you're gonna be bringin' love to Mississippi rednecks.

JESSICA: So, you're just giving up on—?

ROZ: We're not giving up on them. But you can't go into a battlefield without being protected. That's what we're trying to learn here.

HENRY: *(to Helen)* And you. If your partner gets knocked down like that, you gotta cover her. You can't just stand there like a stork.

HELEN: I'm sorry.

HENRY: She could get herself permanently injured, or worse. You want that on your head?!

(HELEN can't speak. After a moment, on the verge of tears, she turns. HENRY grabs her arm and resumes his role-playing.)

HENRY: *(again playing a redneck)* Where you goin', freedom girl?

(HELEN tries to pull her arm away.)

HELEN: Please—

HENRY: You wanna stay in Carthage?

HELEN: I just need to—

HENRY: Stay? Or leave?

JESSICA: Henry: I think she needs—

(ROZ pushes JESSICA back down.)

ROZ: Stay in the dust, coon-lover.

(ROZ kicks JESSICA. JESSICA curls into a fetal position. Suddenly, HELEN screams. HENRY lets go of her and SHE runs out of the room. The LIGHTS change, becoming dream-like, focusing on HELEN and on JESSICA, who watches her.)

HELEN: They're twisting my arm
       Till it breaks.
       I'll never play the piano.
       I'm on my knees in the dust
       And they're laughing
       As they splash gasoline on the
       Blue Ford station wagon.

MALE VOICE OFFSTAGE: Oh, God! Please! No!

(A horrible scream. HELEN puts her hand to her mouth.)

JESSICA: They're beating the life out of James Chaney
       His face like a swamp bubbling up blood
       And they keep bashing and bashing
       And laughing
       And I'm on my knees
       What can I do?
       What can I do?

HELEN: God! God, are you even there?
       Why are you letting this happen?
       What did we do?
       What did we do?!

JESSICA: If I do nothing, he dies.
       If I resist, he dies, and so do I.
       If I beg, they laugh.
       If I scream, they laugh!

HELEN: I don't want to die.
       Not like that.
       Oh, God. You've got to give me—
       please let me—
       Please, God! Don't let me... don't let me...

(A burst of flames. Upstage, the Ford Station wagon (the one that was found in Mississippi) appears, burning up.

JESSICA and HELEN watch in horror. After a few moments, the stage goes dark.)

VOICES: — Damn nigger-lovers!
—You got no business here.
—Nigras don't want you here.
—You shoulda left when we told you.
—You wanna be black? We'll turn you black.

(LIGHTS UP in the classroom. A role-playing situation is in progress: HENRY and ROZ are playing White Volunteers, sprawled on the floor, and the VOLUNTEERS (including Ray, excluding Helen) are attacking them – pulling their hair and kicking them. JESSICA joins them.)

VOLUNTEERS: — White trash!
— Get the hell outta my town, trash!
— Commie agitatin' nigger-kissin' Jew!

JESSICA: You dirty Jew! Jew! Jew!

(JESSICA kicks HENRY.)

JESSICA: Get the fuck out of my life, you nigger-face commie Jew! AAAAAA!

(JESSICA turns away from the group, appalled at herself.)

JESSICA: *(to audience)* I can't believe... how much... What did I say?

(LIGHTS SHIFT: A pew in the Campus Chapel. Upstage, a pulpit, and, perhaps, a stained glass window. RAY enters, followed by JESSICA.)

JESSICA: *(to Ray)* I mean, something took over. That's not me.

(RAY sits on the pew; JESSICA joins him.)

RAY: Better to face the beast, than pretend it ain't there.

JESSICA: But I don't know where... [that came from]

RAY: All of us got a nasty little redneck hiding inside somewhere.

JESSICA: Not me! I love Negroes. I do.

RAY: You feel they're different. On some primal, animal level, you see – they don't look like us. This goes back to caveman days. We huddled around the fire and protected each other from the outsider.

JESSICA: We once sacrificed virgins and burned witches, but that doesn't mean—

RAY: We still sacrifice virgins and burn witches, we just call it different things.

JESSICA: What do you mean?

RAY: ...You gotta face some shit in yourself that ain't pretty. Mahatma Gandhi spoke of 'satyagraha', which means "holding onto truth." But holding onto truth in this country... It's like holding on to a bucking bronco with a firecracker in its ass.

JESSICA: Yeah. ...But I went over the line in there, didn't I? They must—

RAY: Stop. Stop worrying what other people think of you.

JESSICA: But— ! They're in so much pain. And what do we do about it? Act like a bunch of spoiled kids, and then I go... *(beat)* It's just that... I'm really scared, for the

Project. Bob Moses seems like he's having second thoughts about the whole thing. And Henry and those other guys from Snick? They're so angry – angry at us! I know they've been through hell, but we came here... I mean – If we can't work together here, what's gonna happen in Mississippi?

RAY: I don't know, honey. I don't know.

JESSICA: ...Just because Medgar Evers got shot, doesn't make Martin Luther King into Don Quixote. Right?

(RAY puts his hands on JESSICA's face.)

RAY: God bless you, child. You are so beautiful.

(HE takes his hands away from her face, and then suddenly grips his head.)

JESSICA: ...Are you alright? Should I go get—?

RAY: No, no; I'm fine, fine. ...I get this sometimes.

JESSICA: Is there anything...?

RAY: Reach under the pew, you'll find a can. Get that for me, if you would.

(JESSICA finds a can of beer.)

JESSICA: Beer?

RAY: It helps.

JESSICA: You were hung over this morning.

RAY: Please.

JESSICA: But—

(RAY takes the beer from JESSICA, then takes a can opener out of his pocket, opens and drinks the beer.)

JESSICA: You have a drinking problem, don't you?

RAY: Honey, I have a throbbing in my head and an ache in my soul, and I find that a strategic swallow of brew can work miracles, that's all.

JESSICA: What's this ache in your soul?

RAY: Don't you worry about that.

JESSICA: Isn't it something you need to grapple with before...?

RAY: I'm grapplin'. Don't you worry so much.

(RAY takes another deep drink.)

JESSICA: Did you always believe in God? Or was there this moment of...?

RAY: You have to understand, I was raised in the rural South, real Jesus country.
　　...You're a wandering Jew, lookin' for evidence of God, aren't you?

JESSICA: Uh, I don't know. What makes you think that?

RAY: I sense you too have an ache, deep inside. Call it a soul ache. Am I right?

JESSICA: A soul ache. ...God!

(LIGHTS SHIFT, JESSICA moves into a SPOTLIGHT and speaks to audience.)

JESSICA: We leave for Mississippi in four days. There's no time for soul searching. But how can I go if I don't know the real reason I'm going? Am I being called? Why do I feel so incredibly alone? I live for those moments when Fannie Lou Hamer leads us in song, those brief seconds when I'm not filled with petty neuroses, raging appetites, crazy crazy thoughts.

(LIGHTS CHANGE: What follows springs from Jessica's consciousness: half-fantasy, half memory of her visit to a black church. A BLACK PREACHER steps up to the Pulpit. A CONGREGATION appears.)

BLACK PREACHER: Thank you, Lord, for bringing Jessica Kuplevsky to our congregation today. She has heard the cries of our people, seeking their God-given freedom. She comes to us today on her way to Mississippi, where our people live in great fear and poverty and misery, and Jessica Kuplevsky is going down there to help our people register to vote, so that they pull themselves out of the swamp of racial inequity and make their way their to the Promised Land.

CONGREGATION: Amen.

BLACK PREACHER: She's paying her way to Mississippi, saved up from her various jobs. She could've stayed in Boston, gotten herself a summer job, but she's been called to Mississippi. She could've stayed at her college in Cambridge, where the dormitories are guarded by the police, but instead she's heading down to the Delta, where the police work side by side with the Ku Klux Klan.

CONGREGATION: Thank you, Jessica. God bless you, child.

BLACK PREACHER: But to do her job in Mississippi, Jessica's going to need money for bail. That's right, when you register Negroes in Mississippi, chances are the white authorities will throw you into their jails, terrible jails, where terrible things happen. So I'm asking all of us today to reach into our pockets, and pull out a dollar or two and put it in the basket, so that Jessica will not be stranded in a Mississippi jail. Because she's not just going down there for the poor folk in Mississippi, she's going down there for all of us. So dig deep – because Jessica Kuplevsky is digging deep for all of us.

(FANNIE LOU HAMER steps forward and starts humming a hymn, perhaps "Go Tell It on the Mountain." After the first few bars, the CONGREGATION joins in, humming along.)

JESSICA: Thank you. Thank you so much! Your belief – your belief in me, in your brothers and sisters down in Mississippi – means so much. I will write you when I get down there – every week – and give you a full report. ...God bless— ...God bless all of you.

(The CONGREGATION sings, and JESSICA joins them. After several moments, a fantasy version of HENRY bursts in, wearing a green camouflage jacket and sunglasses. The LIGHTS abruptly change, the singing stops and the PREACHER and CONGREGATION turn their backs on her.)

HENRY: Stupid white girl. You don't get it. You never get it. It's hell! It's hell on earth, and your comin' down there only gonna make it hotter. Gonna get some more black boys cut open and thrown into the river. Will that make you feel all righteous and gooey inside, give you some good stories to tell your white friends at the country club? Bullshit! Stay home! You wanna help the black man? Go back to your manicured lawns and your manicured life. Your Peace Corps rescue mission just gonna fuck us up. So git yourself the hell home!

(JESSICA crosses towards HENRY, her hands imploring. HENRY spits on the ground, and storms out. Then JESSICA sees that the CONGREGATION has disappeared. BLACK-OUT. Then we hear the sound of birds.

LIGHTS SHIFT: A path on the campus leading to the woods. HENRY enters, walking quickly, carrying a small branch he's torn off of a tree. JESSICA comes up behind him, out of breath.)

JESSICA: Henry... wait.

HENRY: ...You followin' me?

JESSICA: I just wanna ask...

HENRY: You don't wanna talk to me right now. Dig?

JESSICA: We weren't laughing at you. We were laughing at the documentary. That pink lady, rambling on about how Negroes don't want to vote?

HENRY: Go talk to Roz.

JESSICA: *(blocking his way)* You're the one keeps saying we're gonna get killed. Is that what you really think?

HENRY: ...Yeah.

JESSICA: So – what? – we should disband the whole Project?

HENRY: Just... leave me be.

JESSICA: Henry, the whole future of the Movement—

HENRY: You're not part of the Movement, okay?

JESSICA: Oh, yeah?

HENRY: Yeah. You're just a...

JESSICA: What? Rich white kid?

HENRY: I got nothin' against you bein' white, but once you're in Mississippi, it's... it's not a game—

JESSICA: I know.

HENRY: You don't! You don't know. And that's why this Project is... 'Cause not only you gonna get killed, you gonna get all of us killed.

JESSICA: So why, why did you come here?

(HENRY waves this off and starts to walk away.)

JESSICA: You at least owe me—

HENRY: I don't owe you nothin'.

JESSICA: *(a new tack)* No one was paying attention. Now they are.

HENRY: Summer's gonna end. All a you gonna go back north. And so are the cameras.

JESSICA: I won't leave at the end of the summer. I'll stay—

HENRY: You won't last a month.

JESSICA: You don't know me. I may be a klutz, I may say too much, but there's more to me. ...You're being just as bigoted... as they are.

HENRY: Who?

JESSICA: Those people in Mississippi—

HENRY: *(appalled)* What?!

JESSICA: It's the same damn thing. You create all these tests – Of course we're not gonna live up to what you can do. That doesn't mean we're incapable. – I know, I know I haven't seen the kind of violence you have. But when I heard about those girls, torn to pieces in their Sunday school? I cried, I had nightmares—

HENRY: Not the same as a bomb going off in your kitchen.

JESSICA: I'm sure; you need to tell us about that. But I know – I know! – what it's like to be invisible. I'm invisible to my own family!

HENRY: 'Scuse me.

JESSICA: *(turning to face him)* No! This is my country too, dig? I have every right to be part of this. You hear me?

HENRY: I hear you, but—

JESSICA: I also have great capabilities – great, vast capabilities! – that I have not been given the chance to... You think just 'cause I went to Radcliffe, I haven't known discrimination?

HENRY: ...You better off joining the Peace Corps—

JESSICA: No! If we don't go to Mississippi, what's going to happen? Where's it gonna end? More killing? A race war? That what you want?

HENRY: It's not about what I want, what you want. Jesus! The dogs are outta the pound. They smell blood. *(HE stops himself.)*

JESSICA: What are you talking about? You got something to say? Say it! I don't know the way it is? Tell me!

HENRY: ...Things I been seein' 'round the country.

JESSICA: *(curious, receptive)* Yeah? Like what?

HENRY: Like, I was up in New York City, spent time with some Negro teenagers. They livin' in buildings a lot more disgusting than a Mississippi sharecropper. They go a mile downtown and see white folks with money fallin' outta their coats, then go uptown and the police tells 'em they can't play on the street. Man, when it gets hot up there, and they get chased off the streets... somethin's gonna blow.

JESSICA: Is that why you changed?

(We hear a dog barking, getting closer.)

HENRY: We gotta run— Come on!

JESSICA: Hey— Look, it's just someone's pet. See?

MAN'S VOICE OFFSTAGE: *(calling to a dog)* Come on, boy.

(The barking stops. Pause.)

JESSICA: We're not in Mississippi yet. ...Hey, you know, I have a car here. What do you say we get off this campus, go into town, and get some lemonade? I bet you haven't even been in town yet. Come on, we won't even talk about the damn Project.

HENRY: ....Promise?

JESSICA: Cross my heart. ...Come on.

(THEY exit. Then a BOY wearing a Ku Klux Klan hood enters, looks in the direction in which they exited, then follows them.

LIGHTS SHIFT: We see the front seat of Jessica's car. HENRY and JESSICA sit, holding cups of lemonade.)

JESSICA: ...Now will you tell me?

HENRY: You didn't see 'em, did you?

JESSICA: Who?

HENRY: At the restaurant. That bunch of guys sittin' behind you? Staring at us, and laughin'.

JESSICA: Are you sure?

HENRY: Just because we're in Ohio, doesn't mean people are used to seein'... [Negroes and whites together]

JESSICA: I'm sorry.

HENRY: What are you apologizin' for?

JESSICA: It's everywhere, isn't it? That's why we need this Project.

HENRY: *(changing the subject)* My momma used to make lemonade like this.

JESSICA: What does she do?

HENRY: *(somewhat evasive)* Well, different things. She used to do a lotta women's hair. Now... she does different things. What's your momma do?

JESSICA: She died when I was ten.

HENRY: I'm real sorry.

JESSICA: After that, I was mostly raised by Jenny Washington. Jenny's a Negro, from South Carolina.

HENRY: Your maid.

JESSICA: Originally. Now she's part of the family. She kind of reminds me of Fannie Lou Hamer. She was really good at keeping me honest. A certain look from her, and I'd start bawling. *(beat)* So that town you're from. Is it real small?

HENRY: Nine thousand people.

JESSICA: That's small! Do you live in a...?

HENRY: Two room house.

JESSICA: Yeah?

HENRY: Tin roof, little porch.

JESSICA: It sounds...

HENRY: Next month, it'll be hot as hell in there. Once tried sleeping out on the porch, but the mosquitoes ate me alive. I hate mosquitoes – hate 'em worse 'n I hate... *(he stops himself.)*

JESSICA: Crackers?

HENRY: ...It's nice here. Cool. Clean. Birds are different than what we got. Quieter.

JESSICA: What do you do for fun down there?

HENRY: Fun? ...Barbecues. Lotta drinkin'. Dancin'.

JESSICA: You dance?

HENRY: Used to dance every Saturday night. Martha and the Vandellas, Aretha Franklin—

JESSICA: I love Aretha! I think she's the most beautiful woman in the world. And her voice is like... pure freedom. Shall I put on the radio?

(JESSICA turns on the radio. "Dancing in the Street" is playing.)

HENRY: That's Martha and the—! How'd you do that?

(JESSICA sings along, and soon HENRY does too. After a bit, JESSICA laughs.)

HENRY: What's so funny?

JESSICA: Nothing.

HENRY: What?

JESSICA: Well, you're a little...

HENRY: What? You sayin' I'm a bad singer?

JESSICA: No no no no. You're just not as melodic as, say, Mrs. Hamer, that's all. I like your singing, really. Hey, come on. I got them to put this on the radio especially for you.

(*JESSICA sings, and, after a bit, HENRY joins in. The song ends. Then an announcer comes on.*)

ANNOUNCER: And now the news. The controversy over the disappearance of three Civil Rights workers in Mississippi continues to grow. The Governor of Mississippi, Ross Barnett, said today that he believes the three are alive and well.

GOVERNOR'S VOICE: They're most likely havin' a vacation in Havana, Cuba. This whole thing has been staged by outside agitators, unwilling to recognize that the people of Mississippi don't want—

(*HENRY turns off the radio. Silence.*)

JESSICA: What an idiot.

HENRY: He's no idiot. He knows just what to say to keep the White Citizens Council happy, and keep the Federal government out of his hair.

JESSICA: ...We're gonna change all that. Whether you believe it or not. If you and I can sit in this car—

HENRY: If we got caught like this in Mississippi... I don't even wanna think about it.

JESSICA: We're having a good time. Right?

HENRY: ...We gotta go back. Time for more workshops. More discussions.

JESSICA: It's going to work.

HENRY: 'Change the world, with soul force, 'n songs.' You just don't see—

JESSICA: I don't, and I—

HENRY: *(becoming increasingly agitated)* I been in their jails. Fourteen times. 'Just as soon kill you as look at you, nigger.' We're talking about devils here, see? Look at my hands. Here, and here, and here. Got scars on every part of my body. I been hit with pistols, two by fours, lead pipes, you name it. And all that is nothin'! Nothin'! Compared to—!

(HE stops himself, and takes JESSICA's hand. Silence.)

JESSICA: ...Are you alright?

(HENRY lets go of JESSICA's hand; turns away from her.)

JESSICA: Your hand is still... smooth. ...Does it hurt?

HENRY: ...I don't know anymore.

(They sit for a while longer in silence. JESSICA looks at her own hand. THE LIGHTS FADE TO BLACK.)

END OF ACT ONE

ACT TWO

(JESSICA is alone on stage. SHE addresses the audience.)

JESSICA: For the first time I saw, some scars... don't heal. ...But I don't believe that. They're simply exhausted. And we're not. *(pause)* In three days, I'm supposed to lead a class of mostly illiterate farm children who may range in age from three to twenty-one. No one can tell me what town this'll be in, or what textbook I'll have, or if I'll even have a text. None of it seems real. Before dinner, I went for a walk in the bird sanctuary...

(The sound of many birds. In the area representing The Bird Sanctuary, A BOY in a Ku Klux Klan hood appears.)

JESSICA: What do you want? ...Don't come any closer, I'll scream.

BOY: I'm lookin' for my dog.

JESSICA: What?

BOY: Lookin' for my dog. You seen a white beagle?

JESSICA: You're just a boy.

BOY: I'm nine years old.

JESSICA: Really?

BOY: Next week I will be.

JESSICA: ...Why are you wearing that?

BOY: *(lying)* I'm allowed.

JESSICA: What's your name?

BOY: Bobby. What's yours?

JESSICA: ...I'm Jessica.

(Pause. JESSICA crosses to the BOY and shakes his hand.)

JESSICA: Where're you from, Bobby?

BOY: We're from Boydon, Kentucky, but now we live in Ohio.

JESSICA: And your Daddy knows you're wearing that hood?

BOY: He's at work.

JESSICA: So it belongs to Daddy?

(BOY says nothing.)

JESSICA: Maybe you want to take it off, so I can see...?

(BOY shakes his head. Beat.)

BOY: You at the college?

JESSICA: I'm just visiting.

BOY: You know what they got at the college? Niggers.

JESSICA: Bobby. They're not... (Decides to change her tack.) So what are you gonna do about it?

(BOY doesn't answer.)

JESSICA: What does your father say?

BOY: He says they mess everythin' up. Wanna take over.

(Slight pause. The BOY turns to leave.)

JESSICA: ...Where you going?

BOY: I gotta go.

JESSICA: What about your dog?

BOY: ...It's a toy dog. If you see it, put it over there, will ya?

JESSICA: Sure. Bobby, do you know what your father does when he puts on that hood?

BOY: It's secret.

JESSICA: But do you know?

BOY: *(He doesn't know.)* I ain't gon' tell.

JESSICA: You know what they have over at the college?

BOY: I ain't allowed over there.

(The BOY leaves.)

JESSICA: Bobby. ...Oh my God!

(LIGHTS SHIFT to The Classroom: a training session is in progress. JOHN sits in a chair in the center of the area, smoking his pipe. The rest of the group – STAFF and VOL-UNTEERS – sit on the sidelines. JESSICA becomes part of the group. HELEN is back, but stands close to the door.)

RAY: "Ring, ring. Ring, ring."

JOHN: *(pantomimes picking up an invisible phone)* Hello.

RAY: White boy?

JOHN: This is John.

RAY: Listen to me, John boy. You get out of that house tonight, or that nigger family you're staying with gonna get their throats cut.

JOHN: Who is this?

RAY: You don't wanna be responsible for those black babies endin' up dead, now do you?

JOHN: Let's talk about this.

RAY: *(as if he's hanging up the phone)* "Click"

(Pause)

ROZ: So now what? ...Do you pack your bags, or...?

JOHN: *(as if calling out to someone)* Bessie! Bessie!

ROZ: "Bessie"?

JOHN: That's the mother of the family. Bessie. Something wrong with that name?

HENRY: Not if you're namin' a cow.

ROZ: It's fine. I'm Bessie. *(Crossing to John; assuming the role.)* Mr. John, you look white as a sheet. You see another garden snake?

(The GROUP laughs.)

JOHN: I just got a call from someone... He says if I don't clear out by midnight, they're going to...

ROZ: Oh, Lord.

JOHN: Do you have any idea who...?

ROZ: *(shakes her head.)* Could be twenty different men make a call like that.

JOHN: When does Mr. Harper get back?

ROZ: 'Round midnight.

JOHN: I think... for the time being, it's probably best that I—

ROZ: Listen here, you is our guest.

JOHN: He said he was going to harm your kids. I think I better go.

RAY: *(interrupting the role-playing)* But how do you know this isn't just a tactic, to get you out into the night, so they can grab you?

JOHN: I don't. But I'm not willing to risk the lives of those children.

ROZ: John: How do you know this family isn't safer if you stay? The Klan may be less inclined to bomb a house if there's a white in it.

JOHN: So... I should stay.

ROZ: If you stay, you'll enrage the Klan. Reprisal is certain.

JOHN: So, I should go. Right?

HENRY: You don't ever want to be headin' for town after dark.

JOHN: So what am I supposed to do?

(The VOLUNTEERS, clearly disturbed, talk among themselves.)

ROZ: ...We can't tell you. We can only prepare you – try to prepare you... for decisions you have to make.

(Pause: The VOLUNTEERS are speechless.)

ROZ: We need to stop for now.

JOHN: But –   ...Can we pick this up afterwards?

ROZ: *(somewhat hesitantly)* ...Perhaps. We have a lot of other ground to cover. *(Beat. Roz looks at her watch.)* I will see you all at three sharp. Thank you.

(The VOLUNTEERS and STAFF exit.)

ROZ: Jessica, may I speak with you?

(JESSICA comes forward.)

ROZ: Please, sit down.

(THEY sit. ROZ waits for the others to leave.)

JESSICA: What is it?

ROZ: I need to talk with you about Henry. I understand, with all that's going on, the temptation—

JESSICA: We're not... We just went to town. Are people thinking...? Because Henry's not like that.

ROZ: I know.

JESSICA: You worked with him before, didn't you?

ROZ: My husband and I spent six months in Mabley last year, working very closely with Henry.

JESSICA: What happened?

ROZ: It's not my place to share his personal situation with you. But you do need to know... He's on a precipice. It's best that you... give him space.

JESSICA: So, you're saying I shouldn't even...? I'm not like those other girls.

ROZ: I know. Thank you, Jessica.

JESSICA: Don't you think it could only help him to have another friend?

ROZ: But aren't you looking for more?

JESSICA: ...I guess I... *(beat)* I'm here for the Project. The Beloved Community. Isn't that made up of individual connections? And isn't our work about—?

ROZ: It doesn't happen overnight. Or in one summer. Okay?

(Pause)

JESSICA: I'd like to switch to voter registration.

ROZ: Jessica... You want to lower barriers? Try getting a Negro child in Mississippi to see that college is not just a country club for white folks. ...I'm late for a staff meeting.

(ROZ gathers her notes and clipboard.)

JESSICA: Roz. Where's your husband now?

ROZ: Mississippi.

JESSICA: Where?

ROZ: ...I don't know. We're not together anymore. You'll have to excuse me.

(ROZ exits.)

BOB MOSES appears at a podium. Behind him is the blackboard with the names of the three missing young men. MOSES refers to some pages, and addresses the audience.)

BOB MOSES: Yesterday, in McComb County, Mississippi, three bombs were set off in the homes of Negro families hosting white civil rights workers. In Moss Point, two more Summer Project volunteers have been arrested. We are trying to contact authorities there.
    And this unconfirmed report: ...In Ruleville, some white people drove through the Negro neighborhood and threw some candy out their window. One child who ate the candy is reported to have died.

(LIGHTS DOWN on BOB MOSES.)

JESSICA: The whole thing starts to sound like a spaghetti western directed by Ingmar Bergman, until I see the eyes of the staff members. Piercing, bloodshot... Henry... sitting on so much. I'll never know what. And yet... I need to know. I'm meant to know. *(This last remark catches her by surprise. Pause.)* I watched him today, talking with Bob Moses on the porch of Presser Hall.

(Additional LIGHTS on Porch. BOB MOSES is sitting on a bench. Enter HENRY.)

HENRY: These kids... No way these kids gonna be ready by Saturday.

BOB MOSES: ...So what do you think we should—?

HENRY: We gotta do somethin'! Somethin' that's gonna work, that isn't gonna take a hundred years. 'Cause we don't have a hundred years. We may not even have a whole summer. ...There's people out there... talkin' 'bout... a different way. There's a group, gone into the woods. They're planning quick actions against the Klan, like South American guerilla fighters—

BOB MOSES: How do you know about this?

HENRY: I got a letter from Linwood.

BOB MOSES: You mean Roz's husband? Where is he?

HENRY: Somewhere near McComb. He says they have twenty men. Asked me to come down and join them.

BOB MOSES: Henry. ...Henry. You're doing important work here.

HENRY: What work? I don't see nothin' good coming out of this. *(pause)* We got to *do* something, man. Now.

BOB MOSES: You think I don't hear what's goin' down? Here, and down there? You think I ever stop hearing it? I have blood on my hands too! If one more person gets killed, I.... But I can't conceive of an alternative. Guerilla war in the Delta? That's—

HENRY: We already in a war!

BOB MOSES: Do you really believe Linwood's guerilla play-acting is going to spark a revolution? You think the sharecroppers in Mabley are going to take up guns? What Mississippi needs is—

HENRY: I'm tellin' you man, this Project ain't gonna work.

BOB MOSES: ...Maybe...

HENRY: What? ...What?!

(BOB MOSES, wrapped in thought, says nothing. HENRY abruptly exits.)

BOB MOSES: Henry! *(alone)* ....Maybe...

(BOB MOSES presses his fingers into his forehead.)

JESSICA: Don't give up, Bob Moses,
Don't give up.
You see something beyond today.
At least you're trying to.
If only I could sleep
I could dream.

(In dream-like lighting, JESSICA watches as FANNIE LOU HAMER appears and sings to Bob Moses the following lines from the traditional hymn, "I Want Jesus to Walk With Me".)

FANNIE LOU HAMER: In my trial, Lord, walk with me
In my trial, Lord, walk with me
When the shades of life are falling
Lord, I want Jesus to walk with me.

(LIGHTS cross fade to SEVERAL VOLUNTEERS standing in line in the Cafeteria.)

VOLUNTEERS: *(severally)* —Am I being a prima donna?
—No! We go down there in two days.
—All I asked was, 'how do you decide where to send us?'
—I've just about had it.
—Hey: Think about what they're coping with.
—Does that give 'em the right to call me a white bitch?
—If they think so little of us
—What are we supposed to accomplish down there?

(The VOLUNTEERS all echo this question.

LIGHTS SHIFT: The Woods. HENRY enters, walking quickly. Soon, JESSICA enters behind him. HENRY whirls around.)

HENRY: You followin' me again?

JESSICA: You could've at least said something.

HENRY: I'm not the supervisor of every Negro on this project.

JESSICA: They respect you. Why don't you speak up?

HENRY: I ain't in the mood for talkin'.

JESSICA: Is it unreasonable to ask what our assignments are?

(HENRY walks away from her.)

JESSICA: Hey! Come back here.

(JESSICA goes after him and grabs his arm.)

JESSICA: Please. We have to talk.

HENRY: No more talkin'! I'm sick-a talk, talk, talk!

JESSICA: Then let me just walk with you. I won't say a word.

HENRY: Why? ...I told you: leave me be. ....What do you want?

(JESSICA gestures that she's not going to talk. HENRY shakes his head, turns around and starts walking, really fast. JESSICA follows. THEY exit, then soon reappear in-

Another part of the woods. HENRY is still several paces ahead of JESSICA. HENRY jumps over a log. Soon after, JESSICA jumps over it, trips and falls on her face. HENRY keeps walking a few seconds, then turns around to see what happened.)

HENRY: ...You alright?

(JESSICA nods, but has gotten some scrapes. HENRY goes to her and helps her up.)

JESSICA: Thank you.

HENRY: *(referring to her hand:)* ...Lemme see. ...You wanna get that cleaned.

(The BOY wearing the Ku Klux Klan hood enters.)

JESSICA: Hello.

HENRY: *(turns and see the BOY)* Oh, Lord! Run! Run!!

(JESSICA holds on to HENRY's hand.)

JESSICA: It's okay. It's just a boy. Bobby, this is Henry. Henry, Bobby. *(slight pause)* Bobby's from Kentucky—

HENRY: Let's get outta here.

(HENRY grabs JESSICA's hand and pulls her offstage.)

BOY: Saw me a nigger.
 But he ran away.
 With a white girl from the college.
 They was touchin'
 The black boy was touchin' the white girl.
 And then he ran away with her.
 Like, dragged her into the woods.
 That's right.
 Eeny meeny miney mo
 Catch a nigger by the toe...

(The BOY exits.)

Another part of the woods: HENRY and JESSICA enter.)

JESSICA: You can let go of my hand. ...You're terrified. I'm sorry! I didn't think! *(pause)* I'm sorry. ...Do you wanna tell me about it?

(Silence. Then JESSICA reaches out and puts a hand on HENRY's shoulder. HENRY stares at JESSICA's hand. Pause. JESSICA touches HENRY's face with the back of her hand. THEY look at each other.)

HENRY: Man...

JESSICA: What?

HENRY: You some piece of work.

JESSICA: There's nothing to be scared of. Not here. You know?

HENRY: Yeah.

(HENRY turns away from her. Pause.)

JESSICA: Have you ever been with a white girl? *(beat)* I'm just asking.

HENRY: You're nuts.

JESSICA: You think you're normal? ...You're so different than all of them. Are you religious?

HENRY: No.

JESSICA: Why not?

HENRY: ...I gave all that up.

JESSICA: How come?

HENRY: Seems like it just keeps my people down.

JESSICA: Doesn't keep down Fannie Lou Hamer.

HENRY: I love Miz Hamer like she's my Momma, but I ain't gonna say no prayer for Senator Eastland. That's just sick.

JESSICA: I think it's courageous.

HENRY: You know what's under those white hoods? You think there's a heart in there, that's gonna melt 'cause you love 'em? All that's in there, I'm tellin' you, is the devil.

JESSICA: Thought you weren't religious. ...You know, I think you're a bad actor. Trying to convince everyone you're a bad ass Negro, but I know you're not. I think you need to be brave enough to be what you truly are.

HENRY: And what is that?

JESSICA: A really sweet, smart country boy.

HENRY: Boy?

JESSICA: Raised by a good Momma, who took you to Church. In a small American town, where people look out for each other.

HENRY: And hide under the bed every time a car drives by. I can't wait for the day you spend a night in my town. That's really gonna be somethin'. No shower, no telephone, no little fans keepin' you cool in every room. And lots of mosquitoes – you gonna love them. You could talk to them about how much you love 'em!

JESSICA: See? You're funny. ...I'd like to be assigned to Clarksdale. I think we could work well together, really well. What do you say?

HENRY: I think I'd rather work with a mosquito.

JESSICA: Hey!

(JESSICA playfully slaps his shoulder. They look at each other. HENRY moves to her and kisses her; they embrace. The LIGHTS slowly fade. We hear a Blues instrumental.

LIGHTS UP on area representing JESSICA's dorm room. JESSICA addresses the audience.)

JESSICA: I know I sound like a silly college girl, but I swear, this was something else. Like we were transported back in time, peeling away each decade, each century. He'd never been with a white girl before; I think this was important. Intense! These layers of fear, and respect, and strangeness. Skin. Soft, but... it does feel different. He's so fascinated, both reverent and wild at the same time. And then, at a certain point, he looked into my eyes, looked so sad, yet also on fire, and I felt... I'm embarrassed to say this. I felt Sacred. I was sacred to him.

...No, not because I'm white! And I'm not just wishing this. He can be... free, with me. We'd freed each other. For a few precious moments.

And then we walked back to campus. Tried to act professional. Hip. But I think everyone knows. And I don't care. I think it's wonderful!

At Kumler Chapel, there was a wedding, a couple from the town. I thought, what if that were us?

(Fantasy: The Wedding of JESSICA and HENRY. A MISSISSIPPI BAPTIST MINISTER appears at the Pulpit, begins speaking. HENRY and JESSICA face him, hold hands. A multi-racial CONGREGATION looks on.)

MINISTER: This marriage is more than just the union of a man and a woman.
    This marriage is a testament to love, love which transcendeth the color of a person's skin, love which heals the deep wounds of history, love that allows all of us and each of us to see – God's love does not discriminate—

CONGREGATION: You tell it, brother!

MINISTER: God's love does not respect segregation—

CONGREGATION: That's right!

MINISTER: The love of God – the selfless, sacrificing, bottomless love of our Savior, Jesus Christ – is available to each one of us and all of us, now and forever!

(Suddenly we hear a window break.)

CONGREGATION: Lord! Run! Jesus! Move!

(*A Bomb explodes in the church. A flash of red and white lights. The congregation is propelled from the church. JESSICA is left standing alone.*)

JESSICA: ...Henry? Henry?

(*After a moment, JESSICA sees something and cries out in anguish. SHE makes her way to a pew and sits down.*)

JESSICA: In the side of the church, a huge hole. Outside the hole, a large magnolia tree, dripping with pink blossoms. It has a brand new fruit: ripe – swollen – only it's not a fruit... it's Henry's head. Beyond that, the river. Floating along the fast, churning surface... a scarred arm and hand, limp, severed, bloody! And, and lesson plans for the Freedom School, voter registration forms, Bibles, books in Hebrew, broken barrels, black torsos wearing only T-shirts, the lifeless head of John F. Kennedy, the breasts of the girl from Vassar, kinky black hair singed white – all of it swirling downstream.

(*Beat. And the LIGHTS start to change.*

JESSICA is now speaking to someone nearby.)

JESSICA: ...Then I woke up, soaked in sweat. And it hit me. What if I'm staying in a sharecropper's house, and it gets bombed? And children get killed? All because of something I did, or didn't do.

(*The LIGHTS have gradually come up in the Chapel. RAY WOODS sits on a pew near JESSICA. HE has been listening to her. HE holds a flask.*)

RAY: All you can do is keep these questions alive. And when the time comes, you do the best you can, with what you got.

(*Slight pause: JESSICA looks at Ray and his flask.*)

JESSICA: Is that the best you can do?

RAY: ...I thank God that Jessica Kuplevsky is part of this project.

JESSICA: Ray, why are you drinking so much?

RAY: Jessica. Jessica. Don't you worry about me. What's really tyin' you up?

JESSICA: It's just... I keep thinking I'm missing something essential.

RAY: Like sleep?

JESSICA: I've never had such dreams... Woke up with this bruise where I dreamed they were beating me.

(RAY examines her arm.)

JESSICA: I keep seeing what happened to those three young men. Their last moments. ...So... [dark]

RAY: Why don't you have a little drink?

JESSICA: No thank you.

RAY: We're all scared. Bloodshed's gonna be inevitable. That's why the earth in Mississippi is so red.

JESSICA: But if we're trained, disciplined – have faith... I mean, you do have faith don't you?

RAY: Here's the deal, Jessica. May I be frank with you? ...I... I can't remember what it was like. To have faith. To have a sense – here – of the providential. Ever since college, everything I did was inspired by this... feeling. I was doing God's work. Then I got my head split open, spent six weeks in the hospital. Get this throbbing in my temple, voom, voom, voom. That was providential too, for a while. I guess I kinda liked being a martyr – real Christian, you know? Then last year, I went to the March on Washington, and I could already see, this wasn't a Beloved Community. This was politics, this was slow-burnin' rage, this was a Civil Rights tower of Babel, with expectations way beyond anything this country's prepared to deliver. And the killings keep comin'. At a service for those little black girls killed in the church, a woman stood up and said, "What you keep talkin' about God for? I'm sick of hearin' God this, God that. It was men that did this, and men that gotta make it right."

JESSICA: ...You're just tired. And furious that Snick isn't letting you into the staff meetings. Right?

RAY: ...It ain't easy, seeing the Movement you... poured your whole life into, turnin' into something – you can't hardly recognize.

JESSICA: Who said revolution was easy?

RAY: You're the one person here gives me a glimmer of hope. You got real shit in your blood.

JESSICA: What does that mean?

RAY: I look at you and my head doesn't go, voom, voom, voom. I watch you in the training sessions – you put it all on the line. Jump first, ask questions later. That's how I was, and it felt so damn right. You know? ...What? You think I'm the only one here drinkin' prodigiously? Those hard young cats from Snick could drink me under the table. That's what you do before you go off to war. You train hard, you drink hard... What? You want spiritual guidance? You're always looking to others to show you the way to God. You ain't ever gonna find Him that way.

JESSICA: *(lightly)* So how am I gonna find Him?

RAY: You're a Jew. You just gotta wait.

JESSICA: I can't wait anymore. I feel – here – I gotta jump first, and hope God catches me.

RAY: Amen!

(RAY offers his hand and JESSICA shakes it. RAY doesn't let go.)

RAY: You know I think you're the finest, smartest, ballsiest woman in this whole damn Project?

JESSICA: Hardly.

RAY: I believe you have potentialities that even you don't suspect. Deep reservoirs of spirit and spunk.

JESSICA: You're high, Ray.

RAY: I'm high on you. God, you're beautiful.

JESSICA: Come on...

RAY: May I hold you? It would soothe my soul.

JESSICA: I don't think it's your soul you're trying to soothe.

RAY: Jessica – we may never see each other again. May I just—?

JESSICA: Ray; please.

(RAY takes both her hands.)

RAY: I see you searching for somethin' – aching, yearning, trying to fit in. But you're a wandering Jew, a wild white heron with no nest. I know, I know, I know what you need. Forget next week, forget that boy – that boy's just gonna use you, don't you know that?

JESSICA: You're gonna be so embarrassed—

RAY: We don't care what anyone thinks, do we? For us, there's only tonight. I would love you like—

(JESSICA pulls her hands away.)

JESSICA: That's enough.

RAY: ...Don't you know, all you are to that boy—

JESSICA: He's not a—

RAY: I've heard them, on the porch of the dorm. "Gonna go tap me some of that white tail." – You're foolin' yourself, girl. I see him: He's not looking at your soul.

JESSICA: I'm gonna leave, before you really—

RAY: You think you're advancing integration? They're gonna hate you in Mississippi – all of 'em. 'Specially the black bucks you allow... I'm telling you, Jessica! — Jessica, please!
    I... I think I'm in love with you.

(JESSICA pulls away from him and exits.)

RAY: Jessica! ...Oh, God!

(After a moment, RAY clutches his head, then falls to his knees.)

RAY: God! ...Jessica!

(RAY gets up and goes off after her.

In the woods. A SPOT on HENRY, who stands, wearing only a shirt.)

HENRY: I am a man.
    And maybe you are my woman.
    ...Crazy. Crazy, man.

    But I felt like...
    I was Sir Galahad.
    or Romeo.
    Felt like I was President of the United States.
    A Negro President.
    ...A man! Your man.

    You is all mine.
    Infinitely soft.

    Open, like a buttercup,
    Sweet, sweet honeysuckle.
    Set my veins on fire!

(LIGHTS GRADUALLY CHANGE. We see JESSICA, sitting on a blanket, buttoning her blouse, watching HENRY.)

HENRY: I could run through the woods
    Singin' 'freedom!' at the top of my lungs
    Not afraid for myself no more
    'Cause I know what it is to live.
    Not afraid for myself;
    Just afraid for you.

JESSICA: Whatcha thinkin'?

HENRY: Gonna need a shower. Again.

(HENRY reaches for his pants, but JESSICA moves them.)

JESSICA: I like to look at you in the moonlight.

HENRY: ...You're nice. Real nice.

JESSICA: Wouldn't it be great if we had a big, fluffy feather bed? What kinda bed you got back home?

HENRY: I gotta get back. We got a staff meeting.

JESSICA: Do the mourning dove. Please.

(HENRY imitates a mourning dove. JESSICA kisses him, then cries.)

HENRY: Hey...

JESSICA: I'm okay.

HENRY: ...You like cryin', don't you?

JESSICA: Do I? ...Never cry this much normally. *(beat)* What happened? When you were...

HENRY: Haven't you heard enough horror stories? Lemme have my pants back.

JESSICA: Those scars on your legs. How'd you get 'em?

HENRY: How do you think?

JESSICA: Don't you want to tell me?

HENRY: In two days I'll be down there. I don't need to visit it any sooner than that.

(HENRY takes his pants and puts them on.)

JESSICA: Is there anything you like about Clarksdale?

HENRY: I love the barbecue – sweet and messy.

JESSICA: Sounds good! ...Henry—

HENRY: Sssh!

(Enter RAY WOODS, drunk. HE carries a bottle of bourbon. His shirt is torn, and he has a couple scratches on his face.)

JESSICA: Ray.

RAY: Oh, Jesus.

HENRY: What you want?

RAY: What I want? What I want? It's not about what I want, boy.

JESSICA: Ray: what happened?

RAY: You gave it to him?? You, you had such promise. I thought you were gonna save my soul.

HENRY: Come on. We're all going back now.

RAY: Yes, suh. Our bright young leader. Aren't you s'posed to be at a staff meeting? Deciding the future of eight hundred Andrew Goodmans? The whole Project is on the line tonight – but I guess that's not so important, long as you can get yourself some white—

JESSICA: Ray!

RAY: It must be said. We follow your lead into dark Mississippi. Ready to die for you. Gave you my life, brother. You know that? ...And what'd you do? What do you do for these kids who are marching into your hell—?

JESSICA: We're not doing it for them—

RAY: Right, right! We're makin' a Beloved Community for every human being on God's green earth. I knocked on the door of the Beloved Community tonight. Had somethin' to tell Bob Moses, somethin' vital. One of your friends pokes his head out the door. "What do you want?" Like he was saying, "What do you want, cracker?" Wouldn't let me in. ...I took blows to the head for Rosalind Anderson, and I was proud to do it.

JESSICA: You're all tied up, Ray. You just need some sleep.

(RAY puts his arms around her. JESSICA tries to move away.)

JESSICA: Come on.

RAY: My head! My head's gonna explode.

HENRY: Let go-a her, man.

RAY: I smell it! *(RAY pushes her away.)* Your scent – and his! Don't ya understand? You can let him up inside you, you can die for him, always gonna be a voice in his head says "she's white and I is black!" Tell her, Henry!

JESSICA: You're just a little sick now; we're gonna help you.

RAY: You think Henry wants to help me?

JESSICA: Of course he does.

RAY: Is that right, brother? Brother man? Huh?

HENRY: Get out of my face.

JESSICA: Henry.

HENRY: We gotta go.

RAY: Gotta run, Henry? Let somebody else take your beatin'.

JESSICA: *(to Henry)* Maybe you should go—

HENRY: You're comin' with me.

RAY: Henry ever tell you 'bout his brother? He runs off, and the Klan thinks—

HENRY: You just shut it, hear? You don't know nothin' 'bout nothin'.

RAY: Got the whole story from Roz. You see, the Klan thinks all them boys look alike—

HENRY: You a sick...

RAY: They see Henry's little brother, and think that's the guy who caused all the trouble in their county. So they beat the shit out of him, made him into somethin' that's not really human, while Henry here... Henry devotes himself to the cause of white poontang.

HENRY: You lie!! You lie!!

(HENRY charges at RAY, punching him in the face. RAY topples to the ground.)

RAY: The power o' love!

JESSICA: Henry!

(JESSICA throws herself on top of RAY to protect him.)

RAY: Oh, Jessica!

JESSICA: Shut up!

HENRY: You're just a redneck! A goddamn redneck! I'll kill you!

JESSICA: Henry!

HENRY: Get offa him!

JESSICA: What are you doing?

RAY: See how good you trained her? What other tricks you teach her?

(HENRY kicks RAY several times.)

JESSICA: Stop it! Stop it!

(JESSICA moves, blocking HENRY's kicks – catching one herself.)

HENRY: ...I'm sorry, girl. You alright? ...Gimme your hand.

(HENRY offers his hand to help her up, but JESSICA doesn't take it.)

HENRY: I'm sorry. He had no right...! He don't know what happened. – I hurt you bad?

RAY: You broke her heart, brother.

JESSICA: Shut up, both of you. You gonna behave?

RAY: I got a beautiful woman on top of me. All is right with the world.

(JESSICA gets up. Pause.)

JESSICA: Things were said... that we didn't mean. Right? Right, Henry?

HENRY: I didn't mean to hurt you.

JESSICA: I know. And you didn't mean... Henry. Talk to me.

(HENRY doesn't know what to say. RAY sits up and addresses the audience.)

RAY: White woman. Black man.
Can't make that disappear.

(JESSICA reaches out to touch HENRY's arm. HENRY turns away from her, exits. JESSICA follows.)

RAY: Jesus died for our sins
And we gotta die for the sins of our fathers.
My Daddy thought he knew what would happen
If a black man ever got a-hold of Momma.
So every time he had a dealing with a Nigra,
He made sure that they wouldn't hold any such unnatural ideas.
White woman. Black man.
Can't make that disappear.
Blood in the river, blood in the earth.
Blood gonna flow.

(LIGHTS SHIFT to the podium in the auditorium. ROZ stands in front of the blackboard, addressing the audience.)

ROZ: Keep in constant contact with your parents, or someone outside the state. Someone should know where you are at all times. Always – always – carry an ID. Also, if you haven't had your photograph taken by the staff, you must do it today. If you're arrested... it may be the only way we can find you. Finally, we must have the name of your doctor, as well as your dentist.

(As if responding to a question from the audience.)

ROZ: ...Excuse me? ...In case we need to obtain dental records. For identification purposes.

(LIGHTS SHIFT: The front seat of JESSICA's car. It is parked on a corner of the campus. It is night. HENRY and JESSICA stare out front.)

HENRY: *(finally breaking the silence)* He's gettin' worse. Can't feed himself. My Momma had to cut back her hours at the beauty shop, take care of him. I thought maybe I wouldn't even come up here, help her out instead. But then I realized me just bein' in Mabley ain't good for my family. They pay for it every day, in the stores, in the streets. You wanna know what the worst part is? When I walk into the house, my brother gets this big smile on his face, like I'm his best friend.

JESSICA: I'm sure you are.

HENRY: It's on account of me he got that beating. They thought Philip was me.

JESSICA: You're blaming yourself for the world's insanity – which is insane.

HENRY: I never did realize how bad a place Mississippi is till I got to be a teenager, and wanted to go swimmin'. Couldn't use the town pool. For some reason, my brother and I would end up standing outside that pool, watching the white kids laughin' and splashin' and playin'. We kept goin' down there, I don't know why. We'd just stand there. Couldn't look at each other... Then we'd go off into the woods and try to kill us some squirrels. One particular hot summer day we couldn't find any, 'cept for this mangy man squirrel that couldn't hardly run up a tree. We'd just come from watching the kids swim, and without a word we put that old squirrel down with a couple big rocks. Before it died, he gave out this cry sounded like an old man. Then we threw some more rocks at it, and just left it there in the dust.

JESSICA: ...You're not gonna convince me you're a bad person, Henry.

HENRY: I could kill a man like that. They do anything, anything and just walk away, smilin'. I can't... I can't let 'em get away with it.

JESSICA: I can understand—

HENRY: You don't!! ...See... before they got to my brother, they had me. I was canvassing some farmers outside town, and took a shortcut through the woods. Suddenly I was surrounded by the... reddest of red necks I ever seen. They were pink with anger, 'cause they heard some Freedom Niggers were talkin' to their colored folk. Five of 'em, with bicycle chains and a big pipe. One of 'em had this big wad of pink bubble gum he kept poppin'. *(pause)* So you know what I did? Jessica? I pretended like I was somebody's cousin, like I was just some sharecropper, payin' a visit from the next county. Started sayin' all this bull jive like... "No, suh, I, I, I don't want to get involved in no politics. My family's a good family, we works for Mr. Reed over in Florence, Mr. Reed good to us, we never want no trouble, no suh!" I'm bowin' and movin' my head around like a wooden puppet, and cryin'... *(pause)* I'd been beaten before, shot at, jailed in the night. But somethin' happened that day... Suddenly, didn't wanna die, not like that. They bought my story, and let me go, with just a kick to my pants. But later, those crackers find out who I really am, and come after me. They come to Mabley, and grab my brother off the street. Friend of the family saw it. "We know who you are, nigger. You takin' a ride with us."

JESSICA: ...Henry, I...

HENRY: Thought he was me!

(JESSICA puts her arms around HENRY and holds him for a long time. LIGHTS FOCUS on JESSICA; SHE speaks to the audience.)

JESSICA: Oh God...
If only I could make it right for him.
But how? *(pause)*
Bob Moses says if only we can survive down there
And work together
That will be so much.
If I can help Henry,
if Henry and I can help each other,
That will be... so much. Yeah.

This is what I'm meant to do!
This cause
This man
This calling
Is me, ours, history!

(LIGHTS return to realistic. After a moment, a car passes by, and HENRY moves away from JESSICA and starts to hide himself. JESSICA stops him.)

JESSICA: It's just the campus patrol.

HENRY: Man... to you it's just...

JESSICA: I know I'm from a different universe than Mabley, Mississippi. But I'm not the same person I was five days ago – neither are you.

(beat)

HENRY: ....You're not ready—

JESSICA: I'm ready to die, if necessary.

(HENRY shakes his head.)

JESSICA: ...My mother was a Jew from Germany. Came over just before the war. She never talked about what it meant to be driven out of your home, just because... But I can see now. She thought America could make all that disappear, that I'd never have to hear someone yell "dirty Jew" or "kike." She carried around this heavy, sticky secret – this shit locked inside her heart. ..."Nothing, Jessie," she'd say, when I asked her what she was thinking. But I knew it was something. I was ten, and my Mom got so sleek and beautiful, and then, her eyes started to see me... And the next day she died. Dad said it was cancer – "cancer cells, invaded her body." But I thought it was the Nazis – the shit the Nazis put inside her. So I decided, I'm going to get rid of all the hate in the world. I'll just love so hard, so good, I'll push all the hate away.

I know. I know it's not that simple. But there's gotta be something deeper than fear. Like what you and I have.

HENRY: I appreciate you, Jessica. But if you was to disappear...

JESSICA: I'm not going anywhere.

HENRY: I can't be responsible for you.

JESSICA: I'm not asking you to. Just get me assigned to Clarksdale, to register voters.

HENRY: Jessica. I don't even know if the Project's gonna go forward.

JESSICA: What? *(beat)* What does Bob Moses say?

HENRY: Staff meeting tonight, he wept. A lot of us did. Can't be sending people to die—

JESSICA: We know the risks. We're not babies.

HENRY: But you are. Plus, a lotta people are sayin' the white kids aren't really gonna change what needs changin'. Which is somethin' inside the black man's heart. Only thing that can change that is black people.

JESSICA: What would they do? Send us home?

HENRY: We're gonna see what the news is tonight from Neshoba, and then Bob is s'posed to decide.

JESSICA: Just like that? Don't we get a say in this?

HENRY: You gotta let us work it out.

JESSICA: But... – Tell me you don't think I could help.

HENRY: Ain't never gonna forget you. The times we had.

JESSICA: Then why??

HENRY: I love you, girl. ...But... It's not about you and me, and a warm feelin' inside – we way beyond that.

JESSICA: I'm not gonna be pushed out of this Project. I'm going to Clarksdale.

HENRY: No, you're not.

JESSICA: Then... I'll go to McComb or... I'm disappointed in you, Henry.

(After a moment, HENRY puts his hand on her cheek, but JESSICA turns her face away. Pause.)

HENRY: Will you write me?

JESSICA: I'm going to Bob Moses.

HENRY: No; you ain't. I'm out of time, Jessica. We got so much to work out before tomorrow. I don't want it to be like this, but... Here.

(HENRY takes a photo out of his wallet and gives it to JESSICA.)

HENRY: It's a picture of my Mom and my brother. It's all I got to give you.

JESSICA: Henry! – They're so happy! – Here: I want you to have this.

(JESSICA takes a ring off her finger and offers it to HENRY.)

HENRY: *(not taking it:)* Your mother's ring, I can't take that.

JESSICA: Please.

HENRY: I'm sorry. I got to go.

JESSICA: Henry!

(Slight pause. HENRY kisses JESSICA, then exits.)

JESSICA: ...Oh, God!

(JESSICA cries.)

LIGHTS SHIFT: *A hallway. A MILITANT STAFF MEMBER appears, wearing sunglasses and dark, somewhat military looking clothes. JESSICA crosses to his area.)*

MILITANT STAFF MEMBER: He's busy.

JESSICA: I just need to speak with him for a minute—

MILITANT STAFF MEMBER: Speak to me, baby.

JESSICA: It's about the future of the Project.

MILITANT STAFF MEMBER: Come on, we'll take a walk.

JESSICA: Please, this is really important. For all of us.

MILITANT STAFF MEMBER: I dig. You wanna give us some Ivy League guidance.

JESSICA: Just cut the jive and let me talk to him.

MILITANT STAFF MEMBER: Oh, I see, you's hip!

(JESSICA tries to move past him to go into the conference room, but the STAFF MEMBER firmly grabs her arm.)

MILITANT STAFF MEMBER: Hey! I told you—

JESSICA: Let go of me.

MILITANT STAFF MEMBER: You can't go in there.

JESSICA: *(calling out toward the conference room)* Mr. Moses!

(The STAFF MEMBER pulls her away from the conference room.)

MILITANT STAFF MEMBER: What's your problem, girl?

JESSICA: Henry! Henry!!

MILITANT STAFF MEMBER: So that's what you lookin' for. Ha-ha. – Henry's gone.

JESSICA: What?

MILITANT STAFF MEMBER: Henry left.

JESSICA: Where? Where'd he go?

MILITANT STAFF MEMBER: ...Clarksdale.

JESSICA: So we're going ahead with the Project?

MILITANT STAFF MEMBER: *(derisively)* "We" Tsh! ... He went to see if it's safe enough for you babies.

(Pause. JESSICA absorbs this news.)

MILITANT STAFF MEMBER: What you want that pimple-face for? Lemme show you what it's really about.

JESSICA: Let go of me— you sick sonofa—

(JESSICA wrests herself away from the STAFF MEMBER and runs away.)

MILITANT STAFF MEMBER: What you call me? Hey! Go on, run home to your Daddy. Ha-ha.

(LIGHTS SHIFT.)

JESSICA: ...I stumbled back to the dorm. Passed some people on the path, but I was invisible to them. Ran up to the tower at the top of Clawson Hall and looked out the window.

(LIGHTS change to represent the window. JESSICA looks out of it. Soul music is heard.

JESSICA moves out of memory, into the present.)

JESSICA: It's one a.m. Everyone's still out. Young Democrats from Harvard, trying to look like Bob Moses.

(A YOUNG WHITE DEMOCRAT, wearing glasses, strolls contemplatively in another area.)

JESSICA: Young women from Bryn Mayr, jitterbugging with Project Directors.

(A WHITE WOMAN and A BLACK MAN come on stage, dancing. We are able to hear their thoughts, as imagined by JESSICA.)

BRYN MAYR: He's gorgeous! Like a Zulu warrior with the mind of Che Guevara. He digs me! I bet his lips taste like blackstrap molasses.

YOUNG WHITE DEMOCRAT: We must be aware of all the implications of interracial relationships. Not merely the question of personal safety, but the question of who may be exploiting whom.

PROJECT DIRECTOR: She is sweet as honey—her blonde hair is so fine, I could put it on a corn muffin and eat it! I'll be her summer Negro any day!

(WHITE WOMAN and BLACK MAN dance offstage, followed by YOUNG DEMOCRAT, who tries to copy the BLACK MAN's moves.

Suddenly, ROZ appears, walking quickly across the stage, looking distraught.)

JESSICA: There's Roz! – Roz! Hey, Roz! ...She doesn't hear me.

(JESSICA watches ROZ watching the dancing STAFF and VOLUNTEERS. We hear ROZ's thoughts.)

ROZ: Like they're dancing 'round the golden calf,
Not thinking about tomorrow.
Too numb to envision Andy, Mickey, James,
and all the others.
My husband has taken up the shotgun,
and dear Henry aches to join him.
Ray Woods has lost his mind
And the super-Snicks in the cafeteria
want to throw white people out of the Movement!
What happened? What happened?
Darkness I can face;
For the cause of freedom
I can accept death.
But... I never expected... madness!

(ROZ flees.)

JESSICA: Oh, Roz! ...Poor Roz. –There's that reporter from *Look* magazine... pursuing a Phys Ed major from Illinois.

(ILLINOIS GIRL appears, followed by REPORTER, with camera.)

REPORTER: *(to the audience)* She's the one! All-American, smartly coiffed, modest yet fashionable, innocent yet determined, brave though fully aware of the dangers that lurk ahead. *(to the Girl)* Excuse me, Miss? We'd like to put you on the cover of *Look* Magazine.

ILLINOIS GIRL: Why aren't you taking pictures of people from Snick? Or that farmer, who came up from Mississippi?

REPORTER: They're not our story – you are.

(REPORTER points his camera at ILLINOIS GIRL. GIRL exits, followed by REPORTER.)

JESSICA: Maybe Henry's right. Maybe we're just one big distraction.
(We now hear folk music.)
...Just kids. Little kids pretending... "I'm so hip, so free. Please notice me."

(Enter A JITTERY VOLUNTEER.)

JITTERY VOLUNTEER: *(to himself)* What am I doing here? This is nuts! I don't even know where they're sending me— *(Suddenly putting a brave face on for someone offstage.)*
– Hey, man, how are ya? *(The Offstage Colleague moves on, and the Volunteer drops his cheerful mask.)* Oh, God. If I get arrested, I'm gonna shit my pants! ...I can't do this!

(JITTERY VOLUNTEER flees. Folk music stops.)

JESSICA: And there's Helen!

(HELEN appears. She is clearly afraid.)

HELEN: *(sings)*
"This little light of mine,
I'm gonna let it shine..." [etc]

JESSICA: All of 'em: terrified, or high, or looking for sex. Nerves shot. Even Fannie Lou Hamer looks... wilted. The light in her eyes is there, but... it's just a recollection, of a braver day.

(ADDITIONAL LIGHTS come up near HELEN. We see a GROUP (which includes Helen) led by FANNIE LOU HAMER, singing. JESSICA listens for a while. Soon, the GROUP is seen mouthing the words, but no sound is heard.)

JESSICA: Was it all just... a child's dream? ...The Beloved Community. The Beloved Community!

(LIGHTS FADE on the others. JESSICA is alone.)

JESSICA: Henry... is going to die... And I am going back to Cambridge, to get my degree in... No!!! *(slight pause)* Face it, white girl. It's just the beginning. Blood must be paid for, with blood. *(Pause. Jessica despairs.)* ....Mom? Why didn't you want me to talk to God? Go to the synagogue? Why wouldn't you hold me and hold me, the way a black Momma holds her baby? Fannie Lou Hamer has her eyes on God, but I can't do that! I sing, and try to pray, and try to be good, try to realize: it's not about me, it's about what kind of world... my children? ...No children. Not for this world. ...Shit!!
...I gotta get outta here.

(JESSICA runs off.

LIGHTS SHIFT: *A walkway on campus. Sound of crickets. JESSICA runs on. Coming from the other direction is SY YARDLEY, an elderly black farmer. HE wears an old-fashioned hat and carries a small suitcase. JESSICA almost runs into him.)*

FARMER SY YARDLEY: Hello there, Miss. What's your hurry?

JESSICA: Sorry.

FARMER SY YARDLEY: You was at that meeting where I talked about my farm. Miss Jessica, right?

JESSICA: Right. And you're Mr. Yardley.

FARMER SY YARDLEY: Just on my way back down to McComb.

JESSICA: Excuse me, I—

FARMER SY YARDLEY: Shoulda left a couple hours ago, but I was waitin' to say goodbye to Mr. Bob Moses.

JESSICA: Did you?

FARMER SY YARDLEY: Nope. He's still meetin' with the Snick. *(beat)* So where you gonna be stayin' down there?

JESSICA: Um... The thing is, Mr. Yardley, I... I'm not going.

FARMER SY YARDLEY: Not goin' to Mississippi?

JESSICA: ...Got a call to go somewhere else.

FARMER SY YARDLEY: Well, now, that's too bad. You won't get to taste my blackberry wine.

JESSICA: I'm sorry. I'm really... [sorry]

FARMER SY YARDLEY: That's perfectly alright. We just appreciate that you came here. That you took the time to come here and find out what's been goin' on down Mississippi all these years.

JESSICA: The truth is, we just made it more dangerous for you.

FAMRER SY YARDLEY: Child, I don't believe it can get more dangerous for me. I been threatened and shot at more times than an eight foot bear in the town square.

JESSICA: But even if they get some people registered this summer... What happens in September, when the white kids leave? What happens at the Democratic convention, when they refuse to seat your delegates? What happens in Newark, and Harlem – and McComb?

FARMER SY YARDLEY: Don't you worry, child. These things take time. And each of us does what he can, when he can. Right? There's a lady in Vermont, sent us down a hundred and fifty books – for our Freedom School. I have never seen such handsome books.

JESSICA: *(trying to be positive)* That's... wonderful.

(slight pause)

FARMER SY YARDLEY: My son always read books. Used to walk all over the county, different churches, just to read their books. Went to college in Tougaloo. Now he's got his own business in Jackson. Great-grandson of a slave – my crazy bookworm, sellin' Dodge pick-up trucks on a lot in Jackson. Well, I gotta go. Miss Jessica?

(FARMER SY YARDLEY offers his hand. After a moment, JESSICA shakes his hand.)

JESSICA: ...Thank you. Thank you!

FARMER SY YARDLEY: You alright?

JESSICA: Yes, I think so.

(BLACKOUT.

In the darkness, we hear the sounds of a large assembly. LIGHTS UP: the Auditorium. On stage, a podium. Close to the audience sit JESSICA, HELEN, and JOHN. They each seem extremely preoccupied. Then ROZ enters, looking almost numb.)

JESSICA: Roz: are you alright?

ROZ: ...I don't know.

JESSICA: Um, this morning in town I found some books for the freedom school. A good biography of Du Bois—

ROZ: I just don't know anymore.

(ROZ sits somewhat apart from the volunteers. Enter RAY, wearing sunglasses. HE seems chastened.)

RAY: Good morning. May I speak with you after the assembly?

JESSICA: ....Of course.

RAY: Let me just say, for now, I am—

JESSICA: We'll talk after.

RAY: ...Right.

(RAY goes and sits next to ROZ.)

RAY: Morning.

(ROZ looks at him, then shakes her head and becomes even more gloomy. RAY just stares straight ahead.

After a while, BOB MOSES enters and stands at the podium, looking at his audience. He sways slightly, then speaks, probing the volunteers' resolve and readiness.)

BOB MOSES: ...When you spend time fighting evil, you become preoccupied by it. It consumes your energy, you become part of the evil... and terribly weary. *(pause)* The kids are dead. When we heard the news at the beginning, I knew they were dead. ...There is a high probability that more of you will be killed. This is the question, for myself and the whole operation. If you're going to do anything about these injustices, people must be killed. ...I'm tired – obviously; tired because I feel this lack of communication. ...Are you willing to risk your life or not? Do you know what's important, really important, and are you ready to stand up for it? If the answer is no, we can say, 'Later, later, it's too dangerous now.' ...At least some people decided to leave today. I was worried yesterday because no one had left, and that was bad. It was unreal. *(pause)* ...I justify myself because I'm not asking people to do things I'm not willing to do. And the other thing is, people were being killed already, the Negroes of Mississippi, and I feel... responsible for their deaths. Herbert Lee, killed. Louis Allen, killed. Five others killed this year. In some way you have to come to grips with that, know what it means. If you are going to do anything about it, other people are going to be killed. No privileged group in history has ever given up anything without some kind of blood sacrifice.

(HE searches the faces of his audience. Then, HE decides the Project must go ahead.)

BOB MOSES: What has got to be done has to be done in a certain way; otherwise it won't get done. ...All I can really say is...be patient with the kids, and with Mississippi. Because there is a distinction between being slow and being stupid. And the kids in Mississippi are very, very... very slow.

(HE looks at the audience for a couple moments, then exits.

Silence. The VOLUNTEERS are both disturbed and deeply moved by BOB MOSES' honesty. They are filled with the implications of the week they've just lived through, and the summer ahead of them. ROZ looks intensely at the faces of the VOLUNTEERS. Then SHE begins singing a freedom song, such as "They Say That Freedom is a Constant Struggle."
Soon the others join in; we hear several hundred singing. They sing with their whole souls. JESSICA, HELEN, and JOHN put their arms around each other. RAY puts his arm around JOHN. Then ROZ puts her arm around RAY.)

ROZ: *(sings)*
"They say that freedom is a constant struggle.
They say that freedom is a constant struggle.
They say that freedom is a constant struggle.
Oh, Lord, we've struggled so long,
We must be free, we must be free." [etc.]

(JESSICA comes forward and speaks toward the audience. During this, ROZ hums the song.)

JESSICA: Suddenly, there weren't a thousand questions bouncing around my mind.
    For a few moments – the best moments of my life! – all I saw was love. The love in John, Helen, Ray, Roz, Bob Moses, Henry! ...and James Chaney, Andy Goodman, Mickey Schwerner, filling the room and spilling out onto the campus, making its way down the highway to Mississippi. ...Of course that didn't last. The kids are dead, and more will die, this summer and the next, and the next.

(The humming stops.)

JESSICA: This is the century of blood.
The red clay opens up,
And spits out bones and marrow.
And in the cities
Men tear out their hearts
So they can throw them at other men.
And it's not a nightmare:
This is our life!

(LIGHTS CHANGE: VOLUNTEERS and STAFF come downstage, severally.)

VOLUNTEERS and STAFF: —We did it.
—We got through the week!
—We're going to Mississippi.
—Natchez
—Laurel
—McComb
—Flora?
—Carthage
—Tupelo!
—Greenwood
—Itta Bena
—Clarksdale
—Gonna get some folks registered.
—Transform Presidential politics
—Teach some farm kids their African heritage.
—Sing songs that will change everything.

VOLUNTEERS, including JESSICA: *(together)*
If we can just get down there
Alive
And live and work with our brothers and sisters,
That will be so much.

HELEN: James Chaney, Andrew Goodman, Mickey Schwerner
live on inside of us
live on

JESSICA: I may die down there.
I have no idea what that would be like.
I'm just twenty-one.
But I do know this:
I'm part of something;
Something big, and bloody, and beautiful;
something beyond me.
Are we talking God here?
...God knows.
But... this is my life, my country, my time
And it doesn't have to be like all the other times.
I say, the nightmare ends now!

(JESSICA turns, crosses her arms, and extends her hands; starts singing "Oh, Freedom." EVERYONE joins in the song, forms a circle and holds hands. THE LIGHTS FADE.)

END OF PLAY

Playwright Bio

Adam Kraar's work includes a quartet of plays about American families living in Asia.

His plays have been produced and/or developed at Primary Stages, The Public Theatre, Theatreworks U.S.A., The New Group, N.Y. Theatre Workshop, Cherry Lane, LaMama, Geva, Performance Network, Alliance Repertory and many others. Fellowships from: Manhattan Theatre Club, Millay Colony, New River Dramatists and Sewanee Writers' Conference. Adam's plays are published by Dramatic Publishing, Smith & Kraus, and Applause Books (including five *BEST AMERICAN SHORT PLAYS* anthologies).

Recent work includes *EMPIRE OF THE TREES* (Wizard Oil Productions at Abingdon Theatre; NY Innovative Theatre Awards' Outstanding Script Nominee); *NEW WORLD RHAPSODY* (Manhattan Theatre Club commission); *THE SPIRIT HOUSE* (Performance Network); *THE ABANDONED EL* (Illinois Theatre Center); *WILD TERRAIN* (EST Marathon of One-Act Plays) and *FREEDOM HIGH* (Queens Theatre in the Park).

Adam is a Core Alumnus of The Playwrights' Center and a member of Ensemble Studio Theatre. He was previously a Playwrights' Workshop Fellow at the Lark Play Development Center, a Featured Artist at the Last Frontier Theatre Conference, and was twice a resident playwright at the Inge Center for the Arts.

Adam grew up in India, Thailand, Singapore and the U.S. He earned an M.F.A. at Columbia University, has taught at the University of Rochester, Adelphi University, Hampshire College and NY Institute of Technology, and lives in Brooklyn with his wife, Karen.

www.adamkraar.com

NOTES

NOTES

www.ingramcontent.com/pod-product-compliance
Lightning Source LLC
Chambersburg PA
CBHW071721040426
42446CB00011B/2159